Dark Psychology and Forbidden Manipulation

Discover Secret Techniques for Mental Domination and Emotional Blackmail Using Subliminal Persuasion, Dark NLP, Deception, and Mind Control

By

Henry Wood

© COPYRIGHT 2021 BY HENRY WOOD ALL RIGHTS RESERVED.

This document is geared towards providing exact and reliable information with regards to the topic and issue covered. The publication is sold with the idea that the publisher is not required to render accounting, officially permitted, or otherwise, qualified services. If advice is necessary, legal or professional, a practiced individual in the profession should be ordered.

From a Declaration of Principles which was accepted and approved equally by a Committee of the American Bar Association and a Committee of Publishers and Associations.

In no way is it legal to reproduce, duplicate, or transmit any part of this document in either electronic means or in printed format. Recording of this publication is strictly prohibited and any storage of this document is not allowed unless with written permission from the publisher. All rights reserved.

The information provided herein is stated to be truthful and consistent, in that any liability, in terms of inattention or otherwise, by any usage or abuse of any policies, processes, or directions contained within is the solitary and utter responsibility of the recipient reader. Under no circumstances will any legal responsibility or blame be held against the publisher for any reparation, damages, or monetary loss due to the information herein, either directly or indirectly.

Respective authors own all copyrights not held by the publisher.

The information herein is offered for informational purposes solely and is universal as so. The presentation of the information is without contract or any type of guarantee assurance.

The trademarks that are used are without any consent, and the publication of the trademark is without permission or backing by the trademark owner. All trademarks and brands within this book are for clarifying purposes only and are the owned by the owners themselves, not affiliated with this document.

TABLE OF CONTENTS

- INTRODUCTION 8
- CHAPTER 1 WHAT IS DARK PSYCHOLOGY? 10
  - THE 4 DARK PSYCHOLOGY TRAITS 20
- CHAPTER 2 HOW TO USE DARK PSYCHOLOGY IN YOUR LIFE 27
  - First Step in Darkness to Discover Your Share Of Shade 28
- CHAPTER 3 WHAT IS FORBIDDEN MANIPULATION? 47
  - HOW TO USE REVERSE PSYCHOLOGY? 50
  - HOW TO SEDUCE WITH REVERSE PSYCHOLOGY? 53
  - Conclusions on reverse psychology and love 56
- CHAPTER 4 STRATEGIES OF MENTAL DOMINATION 58
  - Strategic Firepower for Mental Domination of Situations 62
  - Dominate with Hypnosis 64
  - Essentials to Dominate Your Opponent Mentally 71
- CHAPTER 5 EMOTIONAL BLACKMAIL 74
  - Emotional Blackmail Using Subliminal Persuasion 86
- CHAPTER 6 HOW TO DETECT DECEPTION 90
- CHAPTER 7 NLP TRAINING 94
  - Is NLP manipulation? 95
  - How Quickly Can I Learn NLP? 98

- CHAPTER 8 MANIPULATE THE MIND THROUGH DARK NLP 105
  - Preferred systems of representation 110
- CHAPTER 9 WHAT IS EMOTIONAL MANIPULATION? 120
  - MOTIVATION OF MANIPULATORS 122
  - Cause of manipulation 123
  - TYPES OF EMOTIONAL MANIPULATION 130
- CHAPTER 10 BEHAVIORAL AND CHARACTER TRAITS OF MANIPULATORS 153
  - The most effective techniques to use: Emotional 155
  - The Truth about Negative Emotions 157
- CHAPTER 11 HOW TO USE MANIPULATION IN SEDUCTION 168
  - CROWD MANIPULATION 174
  - 1: Get Someone to Help You 175
  - 2: Foot in the door 175
  - 3: Use the person's first name often 176
  - 4: Flattery 177
  - 5: The "Mirroring" 177
- CHAPTER 12 MANAGEMENT OF DIVERSITY 191
  - How to overcome resistance 193
- CHAPTER 13 CONCEPT OF DECEPTION 197
  - TYPES OF DECEPTION 198
  - MOTIVES FOR DECEPTION 199
  - Best Deception methods 200
- CHAPTER 14 THE ART OF PERSUASION 202

PRINCIPLES OF PERSUASION TO CONVINCE ANYONE 203
Examples of Persuasion in Real Life, in Your Relationship, Work, and Love 206
CHAPTER 15 PERSUASION LESSONS FROM A FOUR-YEAR-OLD CHILD 211
CHAPTER 16 Q&A (NLP, PERSUASION AND MIND CONTROL) 224
PRACTICAL WRITTEN EXERCISES (NLP, PERSUASION AND MIND CONTROL) 227
CHAPTER 17 CHALLENGE & IMPROVE YOUR MIND 232
CHAPTER 18 WHAT CONTROLS YOUR MIND? 237
Subconscious Mind 240
Subliminal Influence 243
CHAPTER 19 CONCLUSION 246

INTRODUCTION

In psychological violence, control, moral harassment and narcissistic perversion, we find the inversion of the true and the false. We also find the omnipresence of the arguments of authority based on "truth", the difficulty to believe that "c 'is true', and the omnipresence of the lie which pretends to be true.

It consists of a series of attitudes and remarks which aim to denigrate and deny the way of being of another person, with the intention and/or the effect of destabilizing or injuring that other. The peculiarity of perverse psychological violence, as a way of relating, is that this attitude and these actions are not followed by regrets or excuses. For those who exercise it, psychological violence is denied, invisible or even unspeakable. The negation of the other goes through the consideration of the latter as an object.

The emotional tiredness which results from psychological violence, from the general climate of 'negation of the other', in particular, in his emotions and feelings is reinforced by the insidious and lasting character in which this relational mode can settle.

It consists of psychological preparation intended to subject the other, to control him, to establish a power over him/her, and is similar to psychological abuse and psychological rape.

It is not less than subjugating others, by subtle, repetitive, veiled and ambiguous means and it is in this that they are effective. Under the guise of confidence, of confession, through words which seem sincere and correct, "From the outside" it is a question of disqualifying the other (humiliations, malice), of establishing a control, even of destroying the other. Pernicious and amoral, "with small destabilizing touches" these means are akin to conditioning, even to "brainwashing".

In the victim of the grip, the possible entry points, the possible hooks can be multiple: confidence, empathy, benevolence, naivety, weakness (we often speak of abuse of weakness in a situation of influence and moral harassment).

CHAPTER 1
WHAT IS DARK PSYCHOLOGY?

Dark psychology is the study of the human experience surrounding the psychological capacity of individuals to harm others. Every one of humanity can victimize other people and living beings. Although others limit or sublimate this phenomenon, others act on such impulses. Black psychology seeks to understand those thoughts, feelings, and perceptions that lead to human predatory behavior. Dark Psychology assumes that this production is intentional and has a rational and goal-oriented motivation 99.99% of the time. Under Dark Psychology, the remaining 0.01% is the brutal victimization of others without teleological intention or reasonably defined by evolutionary science or religious dogma.

Over the next century, iPredators and their acts of theft, violence, and abuse will become a global phenomenon and a social epidemic if they are not crushed. The segments of iPredators include cyber stalkers, cyberbullies, cyber terrorists, cybercriminals, sexual predators online, and political/religious fanatics involved in cyberwarfare. Just as Dark Psychology treats all criminal/deviant activity on a spectrum of severity and motive, iPredators' philosophy fits the same paradigm, which includes cyber violence, harassment, and victimization through ICT.

Pyromaniac

An arsonist is a person with an obsessive concern about fire. These people often have a developmental history filled with sexual and physical abuse. Serial arsonists are often prone to being alone, having few partners, and being fascinated by fire. Serial incendiarism is strongly ritualistic and prefers to demonstrate pattern actions surrounding their lighting fire methodologies.

Concerned about fires, arsonists often fantasize and decide how to plan their shooting episodes. Once their target is on fire, some arsonists experience sexual arousal and masturbate while watching. Despite his pathological and ritual patterns, the serial arsonist is proud of his actions.

Necrophilia

Thanatophobia, necrophilia, and obituaries define the same type of disordered person. They are people, and they exist, who have a sexual attraction to corpses. The American Psychiatric Association's Diagnostic and Statistical Manual of Mental Disorders classifies necrophilia as paraphilia. Paraphilia is a psychological concept that characterizes a person's sexual arousal and apprehension for objects, circumstances, or people that are not part of the normal stimulus and may induce pain or anxiety. Serious human problems. Hence a necrophile's paraphilia is the sexual excitement of an object, a person who has died.

Experts who have compiled profiles of necrophiles suggest they have huge difficulties experiencing the ability to be intimate with other people. Among some men, sexual contact with the deceased feels healthy and not sexual intercourse with a live human being. Necrophiles displayed a powerful sense of authority during interviews while they were in the company of a body. A sense of relationship is secondary to a primary criterion for the assumed control.

Serial killer

A serial killer is usually a real human murderer identified as anyone who murders three or more victims every 30 days or longer. Interviews with most serial killers revealed that they experience a cool-down period between each murder. The serial killer's cool-down period is a perceptual refractory period during which he is temporarily satisfied with his need to cause pain to others.

Experts in criminal psychology have hypothesized that their motivation to kill is the search for an experience of psychological satisfaction obtained only by brutality. After their murder, these individuals experience a sense of liberation combined with selfish power. The experience for them brings such satisfaction that they become foolish to feel the experience of liberation and satisfaction again.

"The term 'serial murder' means a series of three or more murders, at least one of which has been committed in the United States, which has common characteristics, suggesting a reasonable possibility that the same person committed the crimes." - FBI

The murders also include sexual harassment, abduction, humiliation, and abuse. Other motivations have been described by experts at the Federal Bureau of Investigation besides anger, seeking attention, seeking emotion, and monetary gain. Serial killers often have similar patterns in choosing victims, killing their targets, and disposing the body methods. Criminal experts trained in conduct analysis agree that serial killers have a significant history of emotional, behavioral, and social pathology. While not utter, serial killers appear to be loners who find meaningful relationships difficult to create.

Dark psychology is the study of crime and deviant behavior and a psychological basis for all human beings to discern the power of darkness.

"A psychopath, as psychiatrists characterize him, is morally cold, lacks concern for others' thoughts, and has no remorse." Psychopaths act as if the environment is being manipulated to their benefit, using manipulation and artificial emotions to exploit others.

Definition of Dark Psychology

Dark psychology is an examination of the human experience and an individual's psychological disposition to target other individuals influenced by criminal and deviant desires that lack intent and general expectations about instinctual desires.

Dark psychology attempts to explain certain emotions, desires, beliefs, and mechanisms of cognitive thinking that contribute to predatory behavior, as opposed to contemporary human behavioral comprehension.

All of humanity has a store of malicious intent towards others, ranging from minimally penetrating and fleeting thoughts to pure psychopathic deviant behavior without any consistent rationality. This is called black continuum. The mitigating factors that act as accelerators and attractors to approach the Dark Singularity, and where a person's hateful actions fall into the Dark Continuum.

"Dark psychology is not only our moon's dark side, it's the dark side of all moons combined."

The dark mind contains all that forms our bad side. This mythical cancer is normal to all nations, all faiths, and all humans. From the moment we are born to the moment of death, there is a side hiding in us all that some have called evil, and others have defined as criminal, deviant, and pathological.

It is the person who is not invested in his peers who has the most problems in life, and who most hurts himself. All human failures arise among these individuals.

People who commit these same crimes do not do so for power, money, sex, revenge, or any other specific intent. They commit these horrific acts aimlessly. Simplistic, their ends do not justify their actions. Some people harass and harm others to do so. Within each of us is this ability.

Dark psychology believes that we all can be manipulative and have access to our emotions, feelings, and beliefs. As you'll read throughout this manuscript, we all have that potential, but only a few exploit it. At some point, we all had feelings and thoughts about wanting to behave brutally.

We consider ourselves to be a benevolent species because of the fact; we would like to believe that we thought these thoughts and feelings would not exist. We all have these feelings, sadly, and, luckily, we never act upon them. There are people who have the same thoughts, feelings, and perceptions but act purposely or impulsively on them.

This style of predator is deliberate and has a rational and goal-oriented motivation. Religion, philosophy, psychology, and other dogmas convincingly sought to define black psychology. Admittedly, much human activity is deliberate and goal-oriented, related to perversive actions.

Dark psychology discusses the aspect of the human psyche or the inherent human experience that allows for and can even motivate predatory behavior. Some characteristics of this behavioral trend are, in many cases, its evident lack of rational motivation, its universality, and its lack of predictability. Dark psychology assumes that this universal human condition is different or an extension of evolution. Let's look at some very basic principles of evolution. First of all, consider that we have evolved from other animals and that we are currently the model for all animal life. Our frontal lobe allowed us to become the apex creature. Now suppose that being superior creatures does not completely distance us from our animal instincts and predatory nature.

"The greater the feeling of inferiority that is felt, the more powerful is the desire to conquer, and the more violent is the emotional turmoil."

Assuming this to be true if he subscribes to evolution, he believes that all behavior relates to three primary instincts. Sex, aggression, and the self-sustaining instinctual drive are the three main human drives. Evolution follows the principles of survival of the fittest and species replication. We and all other aspects of life comport in ways we procreate and live. Aggression takes place to mark our territory, protect our territory, and ultimately acquire the right to procreate. It sounds rational, but in the purest sense, it no longer forms part of the human condition.

Our strength of thinking and interpretation has made us the pinnacle of animals, and the height of the culture of cruelty. If you've ever watched a nature documentary, one surely shrinks and feels pain for an antelope ripped apart by a pride of lions. Although brutal and unfortunate, the goal of violence conforms to the evolving model of self-preservation. Lions kill for food, which is necessary for survival. Often males battle to the death over the rite of territories or the right to rule. All these violent and brutal acts explain evolution.

"Provocative individuals will always persecute others, but they will always consider themselves persecuted."

When animals hunt, they often track and kill the youngest, weakest female in the group. Although this reality appears psychopathic, their chosen prey is to lower their likelihood of injury or death. In this way, all animal life acts and conducts. Many of these barbaric, aggressive, and gruesome acts apply to evolution theory, natural selection, survival, and reproduction instinct.

The theories of evolution, natural selection, and animal instincts, and their theoretical principles, seem to dissolve when we examine the human condition. We are the only creatures on the earth's surface that feed each other without any reason to procreate for the survival of the species. Humans are the only creatures that attack others for inexplicable reasons. Dark psychology addresses that part of the human psyche or the universal human condition that allows and may even drive predatory behavior. Dark psychology assumes that there is something intrapsychic that influences our actions and is anti-evolutionary. We are the only species that kill each other for reasons other than survival, food, territory, or procreation.

Ecclesiastical philosophers and writers throughout the centuries have tried to explain this phenomenon. Just we humans with a complete lack of apparent moral motive will do damage to others. Dark psychology assumes that there is a part of us, because we are human, which fuels dark and vicious behavior.

There is no group of people walking on the earth's surface before or in the future, that does not have this dark side. Black psychology claims that this aspect of the human experience lacks reason and reasoning. This is part of us, and no clear cause remains.

Dark Psychology assumes it is also unpredictable on this dark side. Unpredictable in understanding who is acting on these dangerous impulses, and even more unpredictable in lengths, some will go with their sense of mercy completely nullified. Some people rape, murder, and torture without cause or purpose. Black psychology speaks of these actions of acting as a predator in search of human prey without clearly defined objectives. We are incredibly dangerous to ourselves as humans and to all other living creatures.

Black psychology exists universally throughout the human species and manifests itself as predatory behavior (inclinations) with no apparent rational motivation.

THE 4 DARK PSYCHOLOGY TRAITS

The triad is a constellation of three dimensions of personality which prove to be distinct both empirically and conceptually while overlapping to a certain extent.

The first dimension is narcissism, a concept first developed by Freud and the first psychoanalysts. The construct used here is equivalent to what is found in the DSM-5 under the entry "narcissistic personality disorder," but in a sub-clinical form, according to the dimensional perspective of the DSM tradition (which proposes the existence of a continuum between traits and disorder). The narcissistic dimension is distinguished from the other two dimensions of the triad by a higher degree of the feeling of grandiosity. It should be noted that the narcissism involved in the dark triad is the grandiose variant rather than a so-called compensatory or vulnerable variant.

The second dimension is Machiavellianism. The concept was proposed in 1970 by Christie and Geis and took its name from Machiavelli, a famous political tactician of the sixteenth century. This concept, to date, has not found its way into the classifications of mental disorders, but it is empirically shown to be distinct by the researchers who originally proposed it. Different from the other concepts of the triad, Machiavellianism here refers to the cynical belief that the key to success lies in the manipulation of others (Jones and Paulhus, 2009). The specific features retained by Paulhus' team to diagnose it are manipulation, insensitivity, and strategic-calculating orientation.

The third dimension is psychopathy. If this concept did not enter the DSM tradition, it especially emerged in the final presentation of the PCL-R (Psychopathy Checklist-Revised) by Hare (1991), considered as the standard measure. If the notion of psychopathy already has a long history since Schneider and Cleckley, it is only a somewhat diluted version that appears in the DSM in the form of antisocial personality disorder. In the triad, psychopathy is distinguished from the other two concepts by impulsiveness and the open exploitation of the other.

To adequately define the three concepts, it is first necessary to identify their common denominator: all three involve a strong tendency to interpersonal manipulation, without regard for others. We could distinguish them as follows: narcissism aims to nourish the greatness of the subject involved;

Machiavellianism takes on a more instrumental and temporal character and takes its source in the cynical aspect of the planning structured by the subject; psychopathy feeds impulsively on pleasure and exploitation (Jones and Paulhus, 2014).

Different regression analyses allow us to find other differences between the three concepts. In the samples drawn from the general population, the subject whose score in Machiavellianism is higher than the other two traits would be a follower of plagiarism, but he would avoid all that is of the order of gambling; the narcissist favors the improvement of his image and tackles any threat to his integrity; the psychopathic subject (still sub-clinical), more than the other two, intimidates and adopts avenging behavior.

The introduction of the dark triad concept has created an enthusiasm in the scientific community interested in "bad characters," and this proposal has generated a very considerable number of researches during the last 14 years.

Let us return to the distinction mentioned above between the "normal" and the "abnormal." A subject who scores high on tests that measure each of these personality dimensions may be diagnosed with the dark triad. However, it remains "normal," in the sense that all these traits remain sub-clinical, that is to say below the worrying threshold established by traditional personality tests, and in this sense also that the number of criteria observed using a tool like the DSM does not allow us to conclude that the disorder is present. We are therefore dealing with a "normal" subject which, moreover, does not seem to be grappling with what the DSM calls "suffering." A seasoned clinician might ironically say that this subject is probably far from suffering, rather than making others suffer.

Because of the subclinical nature of the dark triad concept, the subjects affected by it are probably not found in the clinical or legal spheres. Since these dimensions of their personality do not make them suffer openly and serve them in many ways, they do not consult, and they probably do not openly break the laws. This may explain why the concept was not proposed by clinicians (who do not meet them in their offices), but rather by researchers. The concept could prove to be very useful in the field of organizational psychology, however.

Because of the grandiose and planning aims inherent in at least two of the dimensions involved, one might think that the carriers of the triad are attracted to and are likely to succeed in areas such as politics, large organizations, and big business. If ever the impulsiveness inherent in the psychopathic dimension of their personality came to make their behavior suspect, narcissism would come to the rescue to preserve the integrity of their image, and their Machiavellianism would inspire them with cold calculations to get away with it.

Subjects dealing with the seemingly normal dark triad can cause more damage around them than some subjects with a real personality disorder. Most of the time, they will emerge victorious while leaving several empty shells in their grooves. It is finally obvious that the importance of their success or their exploits are probably proportional to their level of cognitive skills.

Selfishness, Machiavellianism, narcissism, psychopathy, sadism... are among the malicious "black" traits of the personality.

These traits have in common a "dark core of personality," argue the authors of a study published in the journal Psychological Review. That is to say, if a person manifests one of these tendencies, he is likely to present one or more others.

In psychology, as in everyday language, different terms designate the various dark tendencies of the personality. The most prominent of which are psychopathy (lack of empathy), narcissism (excessive self-absorption) and Machiavellianism (a belief that ends justify means), which constitute what has been called a "black triad" of personality.

"Over the years, several other negative traits considered distinct, have been introduced to describe ethically, morally, and socially questionable behaviors, which has resulted in a plethora of concepts without theoretical integration."

The common denominator of all negative traits, which they call "Factor D" ("Dark Factor of Personality"), is a tendency to ruthlessly pursue one's advantage, even when it harms others (or even to harm others) while having convictions that justify these behaviors.

The advantage pursued includes achieving its goals and gains such as excitement, joy, money, pleasure, power, status, and satisfaction of psychological needs in general.

Conversely, people with a high level of factor D are generally not motivated to promote benefits for others (e.g., helping someone) and will not benefit from the good fortune of others (be happy for others).

Selfishness: Excessive concern for one's benefit at the expense of others and the community.

Machiavellianism: A manipulative, insensitive attitude and the conviction that the end justifies the means.

Moral disengagement: A style of cognitive processing

that allows one to behave unethically without feeling distressed.

Narcissism: Excessive self-absorption, a feeling of superiority, and an extreme need for attention from others.

Psychopathy: A lack of empathy and self-control, combined with impulsive behavior.

Sadism: A desire to do mental or physical harm to others for one's pleasure or benefit.

Self-interest: A desire to improve and enhance one's own social and financial status.

Resentful bitterness: Destructiveness and a will to cause harm to others, even if you hurt yourself during the process.

Factor D can be compared to the way psychologist Charles Spearman showed about 100 years ago that people who do well in one type of intelligence test usually do well in other types of intelligence tests, because there is a general factor ("g factor," "general intelligence"). Similarly, a "p factor" has been defined to reflect that people meeting the diagnostic criteria for a mental disorder often meet the criteria for one or more other disorders.

CHAPTER 2
HOW TO USE DARK PSYCHOLOGY IN YOUR LIFE

Have you ever wondered why you dare not shine when you are a brilliant person?

It's because of your shadow share. Would you like to know a little more?

Are you ready to explore your dark side, the darkest part of yourself? Are you ready to discover the dark side of your personality?

Know that a monstrosity greedy for power, money, sex, destruction, and sadistic pleasures hides there, deep within you, in the dark abyss of your psyche. But if you manage to tame the darkness that hides at the heart of your being, you will be the regulator of an inner power you have always secretly dreamed of.

Going to meet your part of the shadows is not trivial. And once you feel its presence, even if you only touch it at the edge of your mind, nothing will ever be the same again.

First Step in Darkness to Discover Your Share Of Shade

Your Shadow, it follows you from your birth. It has become so familiar to you that you don't even see it anymore. And yet it influences (in the shadows) your life and your choices in a way that you should not ignore.

What is the psychological shadow?

I'm not talking about the physical shadow that your body casts as soon as there is an ounce of light. I am talking to you; you will understand this part of yourself, which interacts sneakily in you and secretly influences your thoughts and, therefore, your whole life.

Your whole life, from your childhood, is influenced by this part of yourself that you constantly seek to flee without even realizing it.

Just as the only way to escape from your physical shadow would be to live in permanent darkness, your way to flee from your psychic shadow is to seek to live in the light.

Yes, you are like these moths that throw themselves on the light even if they burn their wings to flee the darkness of the night.

But your psychological shadow, as dark as it is, is not so terrible. If you are patient, caring, and persistent, you may even make it stronger. But before making it a force, you must already make it an ally. And that is not going to be so simple.

When has your shadow part already appeared in your life?

You may not understand what I'm asking you... or you just don't want to understand.

It is the first step to the dark foul smells of your unconscious. Putting your feet, there is neither comfortable nor pleasant. But I still invite you to take another step into the putrid mud in this area of your psyche where you never venture.

Now that you are there, that your feet are plunged into the muddy and stinking water of this dark space of your dark, repressed memories, you can observe what comes to you ... what emerges in you.

No, it is not beautiful to see, and I know, you are tempted to run away, leave this page and never come back to this book again. Courage... yes, still a little courage. Hold on because you're going to come out of it bigger.

At the heart of your worst memory hides the shadow of yourself.

There you are... the memory is finally here, in front of you:

This is the time when you committed the worst act of your life. It is this moment that you will never tell anyone, this precise moment when all your moral values have disappeared and when you were no longer yourself. You are out of your hinges, and you freaked out.

This is the moment when you have:

Hit your child.

Yell at this old granny who tried to pass you by the supermarket checkout.

Puncture the tires of your neighbor who made your wife's eyes sweet.

Steal candy from the local convenience store.

Read secretly the passage from your daughter's diary, where she talks about her first time.

You know what I'm talking about, huh?

I know that I stir the knife in a wound hidden in you that will never heal. We do not change the past, although we sometimes try to rewrite history.

During this repulsive, shameful, crippling act (but which you nevertheless committed), you lived this moment as if you were pushed to act by force external to yourself.

But no, it was just your dark side that spoke and, for a while, took control of who you are.

And those kinds of behaviors where you didn't recognize yourself only happened once. These acts that you committed and that made you feel guilty and feel intense shame are more or less numerous in your life.

Fortunately, these moments were rare and of very variable intensity, but they are very real.

And each time a little voice in you has promised that never again, or never, will you let your share of shadows take hold of you again.

It's a great promise, but how are you going to keep it?

Your share of shadow once escaped from your unconscious and is uncontrollable. There will necessarily be breakage.

The best thing to do, therefore, is to calm your shade before it even takes hold of you. And it's not that complicated.

It's time to tame your share of the shadows.

Is your shadow share your enemy or your friend?

At first, your shadow share may appear to you as an enemy. The purpose of this book is to help you gradually make her a friend.

It may appear to you as an enemy because it is wild and will not go the way you would like.

She is like a black and rebellious mare that you will have to tame. I say tame; I do not use the verb tamed here, which is voluntary. We do not tame our share of shadow.

Some people like to believe it and are bathed in illusions by believing themselves stronger than she is. But it is the day when the animal trainer feels too sure of himself that he is most in danger.

But before you get to grips with your dark side, you need to meet it already. Because it is well hidden there, at the very bottom of your being. But don't worry, getting her out of her den is relatively easy ... but it won't be very pleasant for you.

How did your shadow come into being?

Your shadow share is a bit younger than you by a few years. She was born in you when you were about three years old.

This is the age when you started to understand that certain behaviors or aspects of your personality appealed to your parents and that other behaviors or traits of your personality caused them to disapprove and anger.

You have gradually integrated their remarks to build in you your inner criticism, and to deny in your unconscious what was not acceptable to them.

Depending on the environment in which you grew up, and also according to your gender, your entourage made is erased or, on the contrary, very assertive.

Little by little, a whole part of our personality has been relegated to the rank of intolerable and unacceptable.

You have learned to be honest while learning that not all truth is good to tell. Therefore, you have learned to lie, or just not to say, so as not to be punished and not to feel rejected, humiliated, abandoned ... So, you ended up also lying to yourself by integrating into yourself what is being done and what is not done.

You have sought a compromise between your desires for freedom and submission to the expectations of those around you.

You have entrenched your desire for omnipotence in your unconscious, driven away from your conscience, the wild but free child who once grew up in you and you (believed) to tame your inner wolf to make it a domestic animal.

But it is not because these parts of you do not have the right to speak that they cease to live and especially that they cease to express themselves.

They are there, lurking at the bottom of your unconscious, ready to arise as soon as the possibility arises to return to their turn in the light and be for a time, even very short, on the front of the stage of your existence.

Yes, somewhere, deep inside you, an obscure force awaits its hour, waits for a moment of relaxation of your vigilance. To arise and take possession of your being to make you act as it sees fit, unlike your values and your principles and your rules of life.

It then disturbs for a time, generally rather short, your existence.

Or secretly, insidiously, she will take control of your life.

Your shadow always follows your movements ... unless you are the one who always follows the movements of your shadow?

Sometimes your shadow, in a more subtle way, will suggest you act against the well-being of others, but it is for a good cause, she will tell you... and you will believe her.

Thus, a parent will tell his child that it is for his good if he receives beatings from his belt under the pretext of a, particularly severe education. It is to harden him and instill in him the rules of good conduct. The parent will go so far as to tell this beaten child that he will thank him later.

And this is sometimes what happens. The battered child reproduces what he experienced by saying that this education was good for him. Above all, he was good for his shadow, which has a ready-made pretext to express, in turn, all the violence that it contains in his heart.

Is the shade bad?

Morality regards your shadow as a bad thing.

However, your shadow contains the most archaic, wildest, most animal force that is in you.

A cat playing with a mouse is unaware of its cruelty or sadism. The spider has no remorse for enclosing its terrorized prey alive in a cocoon of canvas to devour it later alive.

The shadow is like an animal that does not know morals. She just wants to have fun, survive, and protect herself.

But the shadow in a soldier can also manifest itself in the form of great fear when taking part in combat and thus make it a deserter overcome with shame.

In most ruthless hunters, the shadow can also manifest itself by pity, and it will let its prey slip away.

So, no, the shade is not bad; it simply contains everything you forbid yourself.

And, if you don't mind, we will find out how you happen to deny yourself the best of yourself.

Your shadow is not only black, but it can also be white.

The white shadow? What a strange idea.

The white shade is all the potential that you have in you and that you do not dare to exploit (sometimes for fear of not making... shade with your entourage or a person in particular).

The shadow part of your personality. How to discover it, welcome it, and tame it.

Your shadow share has good news for you. It does not need to take action to feel that it exists; it simply needs to be recognized and accepted.

Quite simply

And how do we do that, recognize its dark side, and accept it?

In a way, it's very simple. Just give free rein to your immoral and shameful thoughts.

Let them wander around inside you like a wild animal in a protected reserve.

There, your dark thoughts can express themselves freely.

It is in your most shameful fantasies that your share of darkness hides.

Have you never wanted to crush between two fingers, like a vulgar chip, your chef? Or maybe you have already felt the desire to throw in the face of your mother-in-law all the disgust and hatred that she causes in you.

An unspeakable thought accepted by you will remain a thought, whereas if it is repressed, pushed back, it will seek to express itself by one means or another.

And this means will not necessarily be a passage to the act of said thought, but it will manifest itself at best by a slight slip, at worst by a serious accident or significant somatization.

So, to avoid this, you should make your dark side a friend rather than an enemy by letting her live her life as you think.

Make your shadow part your friend and no longer your enemy.

Your shadow share is the opposite of what you like to be and how you like to behave. To make her a friend, I suggest you make her a place beyond your shameful fantasies.

The subtle shade of self. Still there, but yet elusive.

As a child, I tried to walk on the head of my shadow. Since then, I gave up because I never did.

Your shade is like water. It can be as powerful as a tsunami, but it can also penetrate in an extremely subtle way into the smallest crevices of your psyche as would humidity permeate the walls of a house. And yet, when you want to grab it, it's as elusive as water vapor.

Hunt your shadow

Your shadow may be the source of a phenomenal power but, a priori, from the moment you seek it will be more difficult to find than a virgin prostitute in the heart of the red-light district of Amsterdam (if you are shocked by the comparison, it means that your shadow has pointed the tip of its nose and that your defence system has just been activated to repel it).

Turn your back on your bright side, and you will discover your share of darkness.

We all, you like me, have a bright side and a dark side. You have always been turned towards your inner sun to conform as much as possible to your life values and your moral principles.

But it is not by looking towards the sun that you will see your shadow.

Paradoxically, by observing the luminous part of your being more closely, you will take the first step to meet your inner shadow.

And finally, it's not that ambiguous.

What qualities, skills, and behaviors do you value in yourself?

What qualities, skills, and behaviors do you value in others?

What qualities, skills, and behaviors do you dream of possessing?

Have you answered each of these questions?

So, to discover your share of shade, it's very simple, it's the complete opposite of what you just mentioned.

Your part of the shadow is made up of everything you hate at home ... and among others.

I don't like people who show authoritarianism, big mouths, are rude, who speak loudly, never listen to anything, and claim to know everything better than others, who do not respect the Highway Code and who are vulgar.

Here, in a few words, I have given you a sample of my share of shade. I say a sample because there are lots of other things that I don't like about others.

Finally, you see, it's easy to discover its share of darkness, isn't it?

That means that in me there are repressed parts, exiled parts, who dream of being:

- Authoritarian
- Big mouths
- Rude
- Coarse
- Vulgar

Now, I imagine you find it hard to imagine that this is also the case for you. And most importantly, how can all of this help you in life?

You will find out in a few moments. But before...

The other mirror of your shadow.

Another way to discover your shadow is at the heart of your criticism of others.

Listen to yourself talk about others because you will learn a lot about yourself.

The first Toltec accord says: "Let your word be impeccable."

But the criticisms that you promote on others are nevertheless a significant source of information about yourself and especially about this hidden side of your personality that you do not like.

The behavior of others, what you blame them for doing and which, according to you, does not happen, reveals all of your pent-up shares—those parts of you who would like to experience the same thing.

And there, you may say to yourself that it is not true, it is not possible. It is impossible that you have in you the desire to behave like those people who disgust you and revolt you.

In any case, one thing is certain, it is a fact, and these people you cannot support make you react emotionally. But it is time to make this emotional charge a force at your service.

But how can you ask your shadow to bring you its power?

Tame your Shadow, tame this black dragon that sleeps in you.

Finally, after all this reading, you may have wondered how it will help you to tame your inner shadow.

Here are some good reasons (and there are many more).

- Dare to allow yourself to do certain things that you have forbidden yourself so far.
- Don't climb everywhere, and you'll fall.
- A little girl never gets angry.
- A little boy doesn't cry.
- Be wise.
- Obey grown-ups.
- Sex is dirty.

Does this kind of injunction speak to you and reason within you? You received all kinds of watchwords in your childhood that you continue to follow today when they have become completely obsolete, restricting your life. Finally, dare to be yourself by leaving the road that others have traced for you by daring these desires that have been forbidden to you.

Find peace in yourself

Others are the source of anger in you; because they allow themselves to do what your dark side would like to do, but your rules of life disapprove of. Do you have to become the opposite of who you are and give up your values to integrate your shadow? Of course not. You have moral values that are dear to you, and they are precious.

Of course, you can criticize the behavior of your colleague, who is subordinate to your boss. You may also not approve of this mother, who imposes hyper strict education rules based on fear and punishment on her children.

But accepting your shadow is not approving the behavior of those who activate it and make it react.

By taming your shadow, you will no longer symbolically bring these people who irritate you, disgust you, and repel you everywhere.

Because not knowing and accepting one's shadow is talking about these people to everyone around you. Observe who you talk about too often with emotion and negativity to others. Is it your chef, a member of your family, your mother-in-law...? It may even be that these people are virtually in your bed because you think about it at night or with you in the shower. After all, there too, you think.

By returning to your shadow, you will free their presence from your thoughts so that you can use this energy for more positive and favorable things for you. Think about it...

Don't let others manipulate you anymore because of your shadow.

Individuals who have mastered the art of manipulating others very quickly know how to perceive others' shadows.

You're not heading!

This is how it is that when one has told certain people that they are not capable of something or are afraid of doing something, that is enough to trigger the requested behavior. Their fear has been so suppressed as well as the shame of not being able that this simple sentence can be an easy stimulus to use to manipulate them. Is this your case?

To others, all it takes is a little flattery well turned to get them to do as they want (like dropping a cheese like a crow in La Fontaine's fable). Pride and the desire to please others is ultimately only a way of protecting oneself from the fear of rejection and repressed abandonment with the injured child in oneself at the bottom of who they are. Once fear and your share of shadow are admitted and recognized, the strings that the manipulator pulls no longer exist in your home.

Stop being a compulsive savior by reinstating your fair share of selfishness.

Are you the kind of "good Samaritan" who always wants to help and support others (and sometimes without being asked)? There too, the fact of ignoring your share of shade has something to do with it.

You will tell me that it is good to help people. Of course, I am not telling you to become a monster of selfishness and to crush others to achieve your ends.

On the other hand, when you exhaust yourself by pumping in your energy to deal with the problems of others, there, it is you who does not respect yourself. Taking care of yourself, not always coming after everyone, may be selfish for you. Do you hear in yourself a voice that is critical inside that drives you to the guilt of taking care of yourself and taking the time to rest?

I like to say that a good caregiver starts by taking care of himself because we cannot help in the long term for others if we do not also take care of ourselves.

So by going into your shadow share for a form of "just selfishness," you will be able to say "no" and "stop" so as not to provide excessive help to people who could ultimately do without your help (but are you ready to accept it?).

There are still other advantages to leaving room in you for your share of shade, but I let you discover them for yourself.

Stop seeing your shadow through a distorting mirror.

I am neither a psychologist nor a psychotherapist and even less a psychiatrist. But during my life, I learned one essential thing: to go to meet yourself, and it is essential to see yourself through the eyes of others.

And how do we get to see ourselves through the eyes of others?

It is very simple. To do this, simply open your ears.

By opening your ears, you will hear what everyone is saying about you. But more often than not, what you will hear is distorted by the other's admiring or disapproving look at you.

Sometimes, the neutral gaze of a person who does not know you, and who does not judge you, welcomes you as you are, without preconceptions, can allow you to take a step closer to knowing yourself. For this, no need for a relationship of psychological care, a relationship of trust and mutual respect is enough. I suggest that you be that person if you feel like it.

CHAPTER 3
WHAT IS FORBIDDEN MANIPULATION?

What is reverse psychology, and how can it be applied in love?

We talk about reverse psychology when we try to induce in the other an attitude opposed to what we communicate to him or that we adopt.

Reverse psychology in love, can education help? Is it fair to use it? Find out what reverse psychology is and how to use it!

What is reverse psychology?

Reverse psychology, is, in fact, a manipulative mechanism that tries to get a person to do something that he doesn't want to do. This type of psychological tactic is generally used with children and adolescents.

Reactivity in psychology is called an individual's attempt to restore freedom of action that feels threatened. This attitude is typical of children and adolescents, who, in the process of building their identity, tend to respond with reactivity, and therefore to disobey an order which, even if they deem it right, do not want to do because it is an order that undermines their freedom.

For this reason, parents very often tend to use reverse psychology tactics to lead their child to a path they deem appropriate. This is, for example, the case of the child who does not want to eat fish or vegetables. The more you force a baby to eat it, the less he will want to eat it.

But how do you make them want? The first step would be to create a dish and a story as attractive as possible to intrigue him, and then, through reverse psychology, even give him a taste of the forbidden.

Back and reverse

But what is the right way to bond with someone? Do we need to use reverse psychology in education?

Ultimately, this type of psychology is a type of psychological process of manipulation. How good is it really to use it? There are contraindications in this sense because reverse psychology uses the other's weaknesses to open a window to the desires that we want the other to hear.

At the educational level, there are two unfavorable points to consider:

The first point is that if you allow a child to do the opposite of what the parent says, you are undermining the parent's authority. Reverse psychology, therefore, opens a gap in another aspect of education.

At the educational level, communication works more than reverse psychology. Children learn through communication and the explanation of phenomena and things. It is possible to use reverse psychology in certain situations, but it is always better to try to have a communicative approach and not only imposed or reverse.

In adulthood, reverse psychology can be used both in the workplace and especially in love.

Although certain attitudes of reverse psychology are more easily recognized in adulthood, there are also more veiled cases that are applied by companies or boyfriends (or ex-fiancés).

At work, an example could be a company that promotes training courses for employees outside of working hours that no one signs up for: one tactic to get people to sign up would be to advertise that courses will be canceled (although this may not be true). This could raise awareness for workers who miss an important opportunity and perhaps provide the impetus for them to take a look and possibly register.

In love, reverse psychology can be used to conquer someone or to rekindle the couple's relationship.

Even so, it should always be used with caution, because in the end, the important thing is always what the other person feels, not what we impose on it. But let's take a closer look.

HOW TO USE REVERSE PSYCHOLOGY?

This psychological process must be used with caution, and above all, it is not possible to always do it with people and make it become a habit.

If you find yourself in a reverse manipulative attitude, you might ask yourself the following questions, to try to limit it to certain situations and contexts:

Who are you using this method with, and why? If you use it because your child is no longer eating vegetables, it may be fine, but if you are using it to try to manipulate a company employee, client, or perhaps your husband, it is not a good thing.

What is the effect of reverse psychology on the person you are targeting? Denying something might cause the other to do the opposite, but you might also not do it if it was more practical.

What is the other person's need for freedom? As we have seen, in the phase of building the identity of the person, or in the case of people needing self-affirmation, it is more possible that they work in reverse psychology (if we order to do something to someone who does not like receiving orders, they will likely respond by doing the opposite).

Either way, we should always be careful about what we want to achieve and not play with the psychology of others, as we may cause problems with our self-esteem and safety—those we face.

Reverse psychology in love

Reverse psychology can also be used in love.

The game of seduction has its own rules, which can help to win back a man or an ex or to rekindle the relationship. Love must never be lacking in the game of seduction for this game to succeed. Otherwise, it will be very difficult to conquer someone who does not have (or no longer has) feelings: we could run the risk of creating a flash in the pan that could disappear soon after.

We will analyze two concrete situations: reverse psychology in a couple of relationships and to win back a man. Keep in mind that these are just a few tips to rekindle the seduction game, but if you need advice or a deepening for your relationship, it is always best to ask an expert.

Indifference in love

Can reverse psychology and indifference in love help a couple who have reached an impasse in their relationship?

The answer is probably yes because reverse psychology can help give others what they don't expect. In a relationship, we get to know each other so well that this knowledge so deep can lead love to routine and routine to indifference.

Indifference is one of the major problems of love in everyday life. Surprising your partner could be a way to get attention again and regain interest.

You don't necessarily have to think about big attitudes or events, but a few daily changes might be enough: like stop calling the partner always at the usual time.

Other reverse psychology tactics include the possibility of never forbidding the other from doing something, but by explicitly explaining the advantages and disadvantages of his choice.

How to win back an ex?

Reverse psychology can be a tactic to conquer a man or to conquer an ex: it can also be useful to attract someone. If you don't know the person you meet well enough or don't have basic feelings, these tactics may not work and may have the opposite effect (i.e., say, repelling the other).

As we have said so far and we repeat, reverse psychology is a tactic of manipulation. So light forms, or the broader scheme of a game of seduction could also be used, but in the case of doubt, relationship problems or toxic relationships and dependence, it is always best to seek the help of an expert in this area.

HOW TO SEDUCE WITH REVERSE PSYCHOLOGY?

Even in the case of seducing a new partner or ex, it might be useful to play with reverse psychology to be more attractive and charismatic (attractive not in the physical sense but a more general sense).

In the seduction game, showing contradictory attitudes could lead the other to come closer precisely because seduction is a game oscillating between attraction and fear.

In this sense we could develop a few points to win back a man:

Look safe: We all appreciate each other's safety, and a safe person is normally more attractive than someone who is afraid, who does not speak or who is too insecure.

Alternate interest and indifference: In seduction, it is important to show interest, but at the same time flee a little amicably if necessary. Body language can also help us in this context. Getting physically close to a person can generate more empathy and attraction, so patting one hand or the shoulder while pretending to be by mistake could arouse interest in the other. But be careful because if this game does not succeed naturally, it could have the opposite effect. And above all, remember that you do not need to stay physically close for a long time, so as not to frighten the other or be heavy. Always remember that to approach physically is to invade the other's space, so you must be careful.

Try to go out in a group: The group can give confidence to one person and can make you feel more secure, even thanks to your friends, who will certainly do everything to make you come out in good light. Therefore, it is not necessary that an appointment must be alone (but maybe next time the other person will ask you to go out alone).

One of the main attitudes of reverse psychology is to make a person jealous and to show interest in another person we are not interested in. This type of psychological love tactic might work, but it also wouldn't. Not everyone can cope with competition with others or jealousy. If your man were shy or uncertain (or not interested), this technique would probably reduce your attempt to win back and would only generate anger or indifference.

These are some seduction techniques to win back an ex or conquer a man/woman, which can include reversing psychology tactics. But let's see why these mechanisms work and try to understand the real reason why we want to win back an ex.

If you don't look for him/her, he/she comes back.

Are you still in love with him/her, even though you have broken up and want to get them back? Wondering how to be indifferent and win him back if he/she doesn't call?

There is indeed a theory called "no contact" or the "theory of no contact," according to which if you are not looking for a person, or if you show indifference towards someone, they could come back.

It happens when one of them is completely sure of the other's feelings, to the point of taking them for granted, and of their control over that person. The prolonged silence and indifference may not make him feel more secure: in this way, he may begin to feel the absence, which could lead to renewed contact.

In any case, before undertaking this seduction and reverse psychology tactics, it is advisable to carry out a few reflections by reversing the point of view. If a story is finished, try to understand the reason. It could be a phase of adaptation, and maybe soon you will get back together, but love could also be over (at least on one of the two sides), or they might not be the right one.

Before the reconquest becomes an obsession, an exhausting search for the other based on games and tactics, try to look inward and understand how you feel, trying to assess your relationship and your feelings. The game of seduction is important and fundamental in relationships, but it is then important to arrive at a healthy concept of a relationship full of love and mutual respect.

Before winning back the ex, try to start on your own and heal the wounds that this relationship has brought you, trying to find out if it is him/her, the man/woman you want, or pain that speaks. If you feel confused, don't be afraid to ask for help from someone or a therapist who could help you in this situation.

Conclusions on reverse psychology and love

Reverse psychology is a psychological tactic that can be useful at times to show the value and importance of certain attitudes that we do not want to do.

Going away, showing indifference, saying no, could allow the person to think about what is important to them. In addition to this, reverse psychology could be a fundamental part of the game of seduction, because it allows attracting the other without encroaching on his sphere of decision.

In all cases, care must be taken not to abuse it, as it is always an attempt to manipulate the other person. Especially in love if we use reverse psychology tactics, we have to do it on rare occasions to rekindle a relationship, or attract the other, but that shouldn't be the basis of the relationship. Love, respect, and communication are always the basis of any relationship.

As if he/she wants to go out with his friends, tell him something like: "It's okay, there is no problem, it's just that tonight, I had prepared a surprise." In this way, the other feels free but intrigued by the proposal (even if it is often applied or depending on how it is applied, this tactic could be close to emotional blackmail).

Reverse psychology can help surprise in a couple of relationships, but we must always be careful not to lead to too direct or recidivism.

CHAPTER 4
STRATEGIES OF MENTAL DOMINATION

Manipulators are among us, perfectly integrated into society. Their motivation is narcissistic, and their method extremely well tested. Identifying the four stages allows them to be better identified.

"We got married the first month of our meeting; everyone liked it," remembers Jeanne. "My boss reproached me for untimely delays, whereas I am punctuality embodied, except in the event of large glitches, it is extremely rare!" notes Julien, night porter in a large hotel. "I stopped seeing my friend Magali when my mother implied that she was shouting at my husband," says Louise. Finding a manipulator, whether a spouse, a boss, a friend, or a relative, is far from simple. Generally, well integrated into society, they have mastered the art of masks and are shameless. Their motivation is essentially based on a narcissistic need to enhance their self-image, and they do it with talent. Often, they are fine strategists who serve only their interests, most of the time, to the detriment of yours. Here's a decryption of their method step by step.

Step 1: Seduce quickly

You are in love! It's simple, and his attitude is considerate, attentive and he is perfect. In love, he fascinates you, fulfills your expectations, and responds positively to your desires. He can even ask you to marry him very quickly. Too much! A sign that should catch your attention. At work, he will sparkle you, just as quickly, promotion and new responsibilities.

Why this emergency? "In reality, the manipulator uses masks, starting with that of perfection, which he uses to manipulate you better," replies Isabelle Nazare-Aga. However, he knows he cannot hold it for very long. You touch his power or his territory, and he can transform instantly. His eagerness is, therefore, really linked to an emergency, that of "getting attached" to his service quickly, before the varnish cracks.

Step 2: Destabilize by micro-devaluations

"You look like a Christmas tree with these earrings," says Michel to his wife. Small treacherous remarks, features of irony, the attitude of contempt, the manipulator turns rude and operates micro-devaluations. These processes are insidious enough that the change is not immediately apparent. You can, of course, feel a vague feeling of unease, which you will have difficulty identifying. "However, repeated tirelessly, these murderous little sentences cause a catastrophic anchoring on self-worth," says Isabelle Nazare-Aga. Your self-confidence can only be weakened. Another card in his game: The repetition of orders and counter-orders. Gradually destabilized, you may no longer think for yourself, or even marry his mode of operation, as if out of weariness. You who adore the mountain and long hikes will be praising the virtues of seaside resorts and organized idleness. A typical case of psychic invasion, not to be overlooked.

Step 3: Sow discord and isolate yourself

The presence of a manipulator often leads to a deterioration in relationships within a team, family, or friends. "When my new boss arrived, I felt excluded from the group that we were forming with my colleagues, without really knowing why," complains Sandrine, librarian. Providing distortions within the team, or in the friendly sphere is almost second nature. "Tonight, when you went to get the chicken, Marie complained that you never returned the DVDs that were loaned to you, you should do it," suggests Jocelyn to his partner. The manipulator has the habit of introducing suspicion with the aim of sowing discord and isolating you. Removing the person from his entourage undoubtedly allows a better grip.

Step 4: Feel guilty

Marc is going to spend his holidays restoring the family home under the influence of a manipulative father, quite easy. "You can't refuse me that; it will save me money, and it will allow us to see each other," argues the latter. "He makes others feel guilty in the name of family ties, friendship, love or professional conscience," develops the therapist Isabelle Nazare-Aga. You may find yourself rendering services that will ultimately cost you, which will not satisfy the recipient. "It's nice to have watered my plants; it must have been very hot so if not for you , my bonsai would be dead. Thank you, Aunt Juliette." There is a good chance that you will offer him another kind gesture when you have done your best.

For the majority of us, manipulators are the biggest relational stressors. Says Isabelle Nazare Aga, "all of these steps can even lead to depression or addiction." Once you have identified the cause of your "chronic discomfort," your next goal should be to stop suffering the harmful consequences.

Strategic Firepower for Mental Domination of Situations

As things are, the mind comes up with ever more complex ways to live. In all logic, reality, and fairness, I can say this as a whole. Life is more complex than a chess game, but you do not have as much time to think or act as in a chess game. Sure, those who succeed, deliberate quickly, and act quickly, but they use cautiousness and intelligence in their dealings as well. So those who succeed use very little commentary and much honest and logical action, indeed fulfilling things. While those who do not succeed use much rhetoric and commentary, then very little honest and logical action.

If you want to be a leader of yourself and others, you must succeed with very little commentary and much honest and logical action. For a genuine leader, life is "the show me state" and nothing else. This may sound gross in some ways, but it is the reality of the situation and the truth.

Your being is a reflection of your values, or how you lead yourself is how you use your power.

Sure, to some, life is a game; to some, life is a serious business. To me, it is both, and to anyone rational, it can be both at any time, one at this time, one at that time, or both at the same time. The best way to approach reality is to be flexible and persistent all at once.

But when thought of properly, existence is all serious business. It is a serious business in that you are consistently dealing with the give and take of energy and reality. Energy and reality are the same. If they were not, then there would be no change, no time and no space. All of those exist, though, and we live in them. So, we have to do the best we can at all times as a technique.

Let me explain the nature of real power. The real power comes from our rational thinking. If it did not, then inventiveness would not exist at all, and all progress would stop, no matter what, and we know that that is not a real concept; in fact, I can honestly say that inertia is never permanent in any way. Movement happens, so we have to go with the flow of time, and there is no going back.

This section may seem simple, but simple things are the most complex in application, it is scary how complex "simple" can sometimes be. Reality is simple, and the application is complex. Reality is where we live; the application is how we live it. It is simple to be in a place, but to do the right thing in a place is not so simple. Time to work, play, and do whatever we need and want to do!

Dominate with Hypnosis

The Beginning, Revelation

Do you feel like life is passing you by, and you are a spectator and not a participator? Are you sitting at the bus stop and the bus just keeps on going by and not stopping? You whistle, jump up and down, wave your arms, and still can't get the recognition. You have been overlooked for promotions time and time again. Dude, here is a thought, you are not in control! You are being controlled. You are not standing out, and you are standing down. Yes, you heard me right. Now, ask yourself, what am I going to do about it? Do some self-evaluation. What do you want out of life? Why do you not have it? How are you going to get it? Wouldn't it be wonderful to find a solution to all the issues that affect your well-being? Well, don't quit now! Don't be close-minded before you even get started. Today is the day to begin your life-changing journey. Now let's break the mold and start changing your direction of travel. No one can do it for you, You Have to Do It. Are you ready? OK, that is what I like to hear. Let us start by learning a little about why we are the way we are.

Are We Secretly Being Hypnotized?

There are people that walk-through life playing the lottery with their future. It is like an anointed few get all the breaks and win life's grand prize every day. It could be they are just living and thinking out of the box. They don't think or bend to every blast of hot wind that comes along. There is a reason why you are where you are today. Because you just don't care, you are flat out lazy, or you believe the flood of suggestive social-economic categorizing that envelopes you every day. Let us take a small peek at what I am saying. As children, we are programmed, brainwashed, hypnotized, if you will, to be a product of our environment. For example, if we were born poor, we are told by statisticians that, according to statistics, we will always be poor because history proves it, and that makes it a fact.

If employed in the common labor market, you are told that you will never make management no matter how hard you work. It is just not within your grasp. If you are mid-management, you will never make VP because you don't have the education, or it can't get you there. Television constantly hits you with commercial ads and programs that devalue who you are, what you own, what you desire, and what you believe. Just think about it, if you drive automobile A and not automobile B, which is supposedly the safest, then you are not a responsible parent. You don't care about your family's safety because you don't drive B. Not taking into consideration being able to afford an overpriced product. If you use credit card A instead of credit card B, then you are not mentally fit to make sound financial decisions on your own. What's in your pocket? If you wear brand B and not brand A, then you are not being a responsible consumer and not being in style, not taking into consideration the poor quality of product A.

These are only a few examples of how we are unknowingly mentally dominated, suggestively hypnotized, into believing that we are not capable of making sound decisions for ourselves. We are puppets that can be psychologically bombarded and bullied into believing whatever we are told. There is some truth to that statement; just look at the morality and the buying trends of the American public. Maybe we need to be taking some mental notes here. The point here is to start being the dominator, not the dominated. This is targeted psychological, mental warfare with your lifestyle at stake. Start thinking out of the box. You are the one that is in control by the power of persuasion and not getting the emotional and mental beating every day.

Hypnosis, Fact or Fiction?

Have you ever just gone to the mall, sat on the benches and watched people? Now that is what I call entertainment. Do you have to ask yourself why people do what they do? What makes them tick? People at the mall look like ants at a picnic with a food mission on their minds. They follow the same paths, one behind the other like worker ants. What makes millions of people buy one manufacturer's brand, and only a few buy another brand? Is it mental manipulation or subliminal hypnosis that we are constantly exposed to? It has been said that repetition is the mother of all learning. If you are repeatedly told that you are not capable of being anything more than a programmed zombie, after a while, you begin to believe it. This is the beginning of mind manipulation, hypnosis if you will. Your average eighteen-year-old watches approximately 180 hours of television and listens to 235 hours of music a month. You tell me where we are getting our mentoring from. You can take that as a positive or a negative.

Everyone is entitled to their own opinion. But if you could take just a small portion of that power of persuasive conversational hypnosis and focus it in a positive way to better yourself, your family, your financial life, would you be willing to do it? People use hypnosis every day to better themselves. They get hypnotized to quit smoking, lose weight, regain their memory about their past, and help overcome a mental meltdown caused by some type of psychological trauma. There are programs of hypnotic suggestion for self-improvement to give a person their self-confidence back. Victims of crime have been put under hypnosis to break through the mental barriers that keep them from remembering what happened or even what their attacker looked like. So, if you ask me if Hypnosis is fact or fiction, I would have to say there is enough proof in this world to say, yes, hypnosis is a fact.

Can Hypnosis Help Me?

I don't know you, and there may be something in your life that you need hypnotic therapy for. I am not telling you to go out and get therapy. The point that I want to make is that it is time that you take control of your destiny instead of allowing every Tom, Dick, or Harry to control it for you. If you are happy being an ordinary Joe, then that is fine, and you don't need to read any further. I apologize for wasting your time. But if you feel trapped with no way out, then you need to read on. It is time for a breakthrough, don't you agree? If so, read the following scenarios and see if you have personally witnessed or have been involved in the following.

The co-workers that you trained were all promoted, and you were passed by. You try to express your ideas at your job, and no one seems to listen. You just can't seem to get anyone's respect. You watch other people get what they want while you are laboring just to pay bills. It seems like everyone in line at the bank was walking out with loans that they had applied for, and you get denied. Everyone else seems to get their dream girl or guy, and you can't even get a date. Does any of this sound familiar? You can probably think of more things that are just as important to you than what is listed. I just want you to stop for a moment and take inventory. You need to approach this issue as this is all-out psychological warfare to gain control of your destiny, and you will not settle for anything less than complete and total victory. If there was a program designed to educate you in resolving the issues that you face in your everyday life, would you be willing to give yourself a chance to gain your freedom? Well, guess what, there is. Are you willing to step up to the plate and change your life forever? Well here is your chance, don't let this opportunity pass you by.

Mind Control and The Power of Persuasion

You don't have to be a psychology guru or have an IQ that is off the charts to follow what I tell you. If you will apply yourself, it is within your reach right now to create your destiny. How awesome would it be to be able to influence and change other people's thoughts? Well, it is not that complicated; in fact, it is easier than you think. All the things in life that you ever wanted are yours for the taking. Learn the hidden secrets that the powers to be don't want you to know. You will be able to influence those that are standing in your way. Gain that dream of fortune and fame. Earn the respect of your colleagues and associates that didn't even give you the time of day before. And if you are single of course, be able to woo and court that special someone that used to be an unattainable fantasy. You don't have to be born with superpowers to influence people's thoughts. It is well within your grasp to dramatically and positively alter your life by learning hypnosis through seemingly casual conversation.

Conversational Hypnosis will show you how to: Trigger manipulations in the brain through speech, convey your desires in any language, and will make others want to help you realize your life goals. You have never been closer in your life than right now to access and keep the secrets to mind control through Conversational Hypnosis. Here is the challenge I will put before you. Do you have the courage to go out and get what you want? Are you willing to step out of the cookie-cutter mold that someone else designed for you? Or are you going to duck your head, put your hands back in your pockets, turn around, and walk away from total freedom and finally happiness?

Review the system for yourself, and it is not for everyone. Not everyone wants to change their life. I just want to see you succeed, check it out for yourself, what do you have to lose? The ball is in your court, my friend. What you do with it is up to you.

Essentials to Dominate Your Opponent Mentally

Have you ever been in a situation where there always seems to be that one team that, positively, always beats your team? Regardless of the weather, who's playing, who has the lead late in the game, etc... you just never win. I can't explain it, and I don't know what to call it, and I think you know what I mean. Well, that's the feeling of being dominated mentally by your opponent.

You can reverse your fortunes if you clear your mind of all negative thoughts and apply some of these tips:

Dominate Using Zen Master Mind Techniques - You can dominate your opponent mentally by applying ancient techniques of the Zen and the martial arts experts. The experts have had thousands of years to train the mind. The Eastern martial art and Zen meditation teachings focus on mental exercises to control situations and always have the upper hand on one's competition. The martial art experts are well known for staying focused and having an extremely high tolerance for pain.

Have Confidence and Cohesion as a Team - To dominate your opponent, you must have complete confidence in yourself and your teammates. It's been proven that a team with good chemistry can beat a team filled with superstars. What is the difference - the mental superiority of a cohesive unit sends out some strong vibe to the opponents that can completely intimidate an opponent.

Be Aggressive and Take Advantage of Mental Mistakes. Another thing to do to take advantage of your opponent is to be aggressive on the base paths, root your teammates on, take advantage of your opponent's mental lapses, and just outright hustle. I have seen one aggressive baserunner turn the momentum of the game around by stealing a base. The next thing that happens is a hit or a passed ball, and the momentum begins to swing. It's amazing how fast momentum can change in a ballgame.

Anticipate the Play – Just as a defensive player goes through the scenarios of what to do if the ball is hit to you. Go through the scenarios that can happen: Are there men on base, how many outs, is this guy a pull hitter, is it a curveball or fastball. Analyze these thoughts and come up with a strategy. There is nothing worse than to shatter another team's momentum by making a great defensive play. It will bring a great boost to your teammates.

Dominate your opponent mentally by being prepared, exuding confidence, playing aggressively, and anticipating each play.

CHAPTER 5
EMOTIONAL BLACKMAIL

When we read the term emotional blackmail, moments, stages of life, or people likely come to mind. Either because of one's own experience—who has never felt emotionally manipulated? Or because we have witnessed someone being a victim of this form of abuse. Are we always able to identify it? And when the emotional blackmail is towards us? How should one act in the face of manipulation? Is it appropriate or not to be tolerant of these behaviors?

If we stop to look around us and pay attention to the communication styles of couples, families, and friends... we are likely to identify, much more than we suppose, dynamics that could be considered emotional blackmail. I think that, unfortunately, it is very widespread and sometimes goes unnoticed, but ...

What is emotional blackmail?

Emotional blackmail is an inappropriate, disrespectful, and aggressive form of communication. A request for change is usually expressed, requests for help, or simply expressing disagreement and complaint, with a clear objective of achieving what one wants, regardless of the wishes of the other person.

The axis of emotional blackmail is to generate guilt, discomfort in the receiver or the recipient, and carry out control behavior on another person, generating obligation and fear.

It is common to associate emotional blackmail with manipulation, since it is a practice designed to influence the will of the other person, to get them to act as one wants and not as they want.

Sometimes this manipulation is very subtle and happens without us realizing it, or when we are aware of it, we have already modified our behavior. For this reason, it is very important to be vigilant, to be connected in the present, to be aware of what is happening at each moment, of what we say, of what we do, of what we want to do; and more with those people with a tendency to blackmail and manipulate.

Emotional Blackmailer

The emotional blackmailer is not always aware of what he does, sometimes he acts voluntarily for a specific purpose, but many times, it is involuntary.

It is common to have in psychology consultations patients who tend to manipulate and suffer for it. They are not satisfied with their behavior, but they do not know how to change it or modify it. These people are still victims of their behavior patterns, which, fortunately, can be changed.

Why does the emotional blackmailer act that way?

The emotional blackmailer behaves in one way or another depending on the environment, and the person or people in front of him.

Their personality characteristics influence. Often, the emotional blackmailer has an aggressive communication style, lacks assertiveness and empathy by not respecting the rights of those close to him. They are usually people with emotional difficulties (sometimes disorders and pathologies such as personality disorders). They also have personal difficulties (insecurities, fragility, low self-esteem, personal dissatisfaction, jealousy, fear of abandonment, fear of loneliness, dependency ...). And very marked needs (need care, affection, and to win an achievement to feel good, to feel superior compared to others, and have personal relationships, sometimes, as a competition or as a threat).

It is common to find emotional blackmailers who have learned to act like this from a model learned in childhood, from their parents, siblings, family, or the closest environment. They normalize certain behaviors, without even considering that perhaps they are inappropriate or could violate the rights of others.

Many had early experiences of manipulation, where they were motivated to change their behavior through feelings of guilt, obligation, responsibility, or fear of retaliation:

"I will let you be my friend if you give me that comic." "I will invite you to my birthday party if you don't tell the teacher about it." "If you were a good brother, you would leave me the largest room."

The emotional blackmailer, in a very high percentage of situations, gets what he wants. He uses verbal aggression, fear or guilt, as strategies to make the other person feel vulnerable or weak and cause them to give in or feel discomfort if they don't do what he wants.

By obtaining a reward, they learn that this style of communication and performance benefits them, compensates them, and consequently they repeat it. This is what we call in Psychology, reinforcement.

8 Clues to detect emotional blackmail

We can all be "victims," but those people with more difficulty in enforcing themselves, those who tend to a passive communication style, with low self-esteem or insecurities, are more sensitive to suffering this form of abuse.

It is important to know that there are different degrees of manipulation. We can find blackmailers who use "their weapons" with all their surroundings, or those who only use them in some specific area of their lives or depending on how emotional they are. That is why we can meet blackmailers who do not always behave in this way.

It is quite difficult to detect an emotional blackmailer, since they do not meet a single profile, but they can present certain common characteristics:

1. They are observant and analytical, and they have a high capacity to identify the emotions of other people, their vulnerability, weakness, and insecurity, and to know with whom they can act.
2. They tend to aggressive reactions and impatience when it comes to getting what they want.
3. They tend to threats when they don't get what they want.
4. They hold others accountable for their emotional reactions and their consequences.

5. They have difficulty respecting the rights of other people, they do not accept no for an answer, and they tolerate criticism badly.
6. They can get others to do things with little awareness of the manipulation.
7. The relationship with these people is complicated; they usually generate fear, anguish, guilt, or sadness.
8. They tend to ignore what others feel and want.

Complying with all or some of the characteristics that I have exposed, does not mean that a person is a manipulator or an emotional blackmailer.

The purpose of this list, as well as this section, is to offer information to identify and detect these styles of behavior, which do not benefit whoever receives them or who violates them. It is important to be cautious with judgments, labels, and interpretations.

Three types of emotional blackmail depending on the manipulation strategy

We can differentiate three types of emotional blackmail, depending on the "strategy" used in the manipulation:

Blame strategy. Widely used in our communication, it is the most subtle and is the type of blackmail that can go unnoticed:

- With everything, I've done for you.
- You cannot leave me like this, and alone, do not you realize that you are wrong?
- I never imagined you would act like this, you are disappointing me.

Aggression strategy. It is the most direct, it uses punishment, and the objective is to generate fear:

- If you don't do what I ask, I'll go.
- If you continue with this attitude, I will end the relationship.
- If you don't help me...

Gift-giving strategy. It is the most difficult to detect, gifts and promises are used to achieve the objective, rewarding or saying that they are going to be rewarded if what the blackmailer wants is done:

- If you accompany me to the concert, I will accompany you to the doctor.
- If you continue with me, I promise to give you everything you want.
- If you come with me on that business trip, I promise that I will go to the doctor to do the fertility tests.

3 Types of emotional blackmail depending on the emotional bond

It is common for the emotional blackmailer to act in

the closest environments, where the personal bond is stronger since he has more "resources" to exercise manipulation.

We can differentiate various types of emotional blackmail depending on the emotional bond.

Emotional blackmail of mothers and fathers towards their children:

- If you continue like this, I'll get sick.
- You are ending my life.
- I don't know why you enjoy hurting me.

Emotional blackmail of parents towards the children in separations:

- With everything, I love you, and you choose to go with your mother (or father) on vacation.
- You don't know the damage you are doing to me. I feel that you don't want me.
- Tell him you want to spend more days with me so we can go to the beach.

Emotional blackmail in the couple:

- You are no longer what you were, and you have changed, you are no longer the same.
- I see what you value in this relationship.
- If you continue like this, we will break up.

How to free yourself, how to face and how to deal with emotional blackmail

Freeing yourself from someone who tries to manipulate you, and being in control of your own decisions, outside of blackmail, is not only a pleasant and necessary feeling but also possible. And you will ask yourself: How?

First, by modifying our coping style, our attitude, the behavior in our relationships. It is a mistake to think that there is nothing that depends on us when we have an emotional blackmailer. Take charge, train your strategies and resources: Take action!

A long time ago, there was a debate about toxic relationships and whether it is better to avoid or deal with them. My opinion is that whatever decision we make, what is clear is that we have to act, change, and manage the situation proactively.

If you consider that you suffer or have suffered emotional blackmail, I encourage you to free yourself and act. Here I leave you some recommendations, some guidelines and techniques to get started:

i. Manage your emotional state, become aware, learn identification resources, and analyze your emotions to help you feel strong.
ii. Work with your self-esteem, reduce your insecurities, take care of yourself, pamper yourself, take care of how you speak to yourself.

iii. Reduce guilt before your possible mistakes take responsibility, look for solutions and learn from experience.
iv. Get ahead of the answers, prepare for conversations, learn from past situations, analyze them and draw your conclusions. This can help you have more resources in the next conversation in which you face that person.
v. Focus on your goal in conversations, don't get tangled up.
vi. "Don't get into the rag" in the face of aggressiveness; in the face of disrespect, in this case, withdraw your attention, go away. Set limits, make yourself respected.
vii. Instead of defending yourself, ask him for collaboration, try to get him involved in solving the problem, ask him for help "And what can we do in this situation?"
viii. Learn to be assertive. Communicate without defending yourself, don't apologize, don't give in, don't give up. Do the opposite, understand his point of view, appreciate that he may be right, you will be puzzled or bewildered and without arguments. Use phrases like "You may be right." "I understand that you would think like that." "I'm probably making a mistake." This technique is called "Fog Bank."

ix. Try to reach an agreement, an understanding, but this is only possible if the two parties are calm.

x. Be firm in your opinions, in your decisions, do not give explanations. If you can use fewer words, the better. Remember that emotional blackmailers are very skilled, and the more information they have, the easier it will be for them to turn your arguments around. They will likely convince you or make you doubt.

xi. Use humor, laugh at the situation.

xii. Do not forget your basic rights, and they will help you make yourself respected and know how to identify when they are not being respected.

Assertive Rights vs. Emotional Blackmail

The right to be treated with respect and dignity.

The right to reject requests without feeling guilty.

The right to experience and express your feelings.

The right to stop and think before acting.

The right to change your mind.

The right to ask for what you want.

The right to do less than what you are humanly capable of doing.

The right to be independent.

The right to decide what to do with your own body, time, and property.

The right to request information.

The right to make mistakes and be responsible for them.

The right to feel comfortable with yourself.

The right to have your own needs and to be as important as the needs of others.

The right to have opinions and express them.

The right to decide whether you meet other people's expectations or behave in your interests, as long as you do not violate the rights of others.

The right to discuss the issue with the person involved and clarify it.

The right to get what you pay for.

The right to choose not to behave assertively or socially skilled.

The right to have rights and defend them.

The right to be heard and to be taken seriously.

The right to be alone when you choose to do so.

The right to do anything as long as you don't violate someone else's rights.

I would not want to end this section without hinting at the fear of disapproval or put another way, the need for approval. Be especially careful with this since it is closely related to self-esteem and the need for affection.

Let's not let the approval or disapproval of others determine us or define us because we run the risk of believing that we make a mistake every time someone gets upset with us. And that will significantly affect our behavior.

The change is in you, do not wait for the situation to take your side. The change costs and sometimes we are lazy, perhaps it is easier to stay as we are, but ask yourself, are you fine the way you are or is there something you can do to improve your well-being?

Emotional Blackmail Using Subliminal Persuasion

Subliminal psychology and messaging are so powerful, and many countries have banned its use in advertising.

You've heard the phrase "a picture's worth a thousand words." So, how can you tap into someone's mind and become the artist within?

It's much easier to use subliminal psychology than you may think, and your artistic skills have nothing to do with it.

Getting Inside Their Mind

Suppose you're a manager wanting to persuade your employee to finish a report one day early. Using one simple word, you'll tap into their emotions, making them want to fulfill your request.

As humans, we thrive on pleasure and aim to repel pain. Therefore, to paint a vivid picture of pleasure in your employee's mind, use the word "imagine."

Firstly, you'd ask your employee if he'd mind staying back to finish the report. Before they've had a chance to respond, you'll follow up on your request with a persuasive statement using subliminal psychology.

By saying, "I know you've had a long day, but can you imagine how relieved you'll be when you walk in tomorrow and the report's complete?".

Using the magic word "imagine" stirs emotion and encourages your prospect to visualize a state of pleasure.

Knowing they're in control and this delightful state is within reach, the prospect will find it hard to resist your request.

The request you ask should be reasonable. Never use this powerful technique to manipulate or blackmail.

The Sweetest Word in a Person's Vocabulary

By painting a picture in someone's mind, you're getting access to their emotions through subliminal psychology. This makes it virtually irresistible for them to refuse your request.

To make this technique even more powerful, you need one extra word. All it takes to show someone a sense of respect, individuality, and recognition is saying their name.

Subliminal psychology relies on trigger words. Why is it that when you're in a crowd and hear someone call your name, you will instinctively turn around?

Hearing your name triggers the mind to react more swiftly and focus attentively. Regardless of whether the message was directed at you or someone else with the same name.

Knowing what you're about to hear is being directed at you, your mind will subconsciously force you to focus and listen.

If your employee's name is John, you could adjust the previous request, incorporating their name.

Immediately following your initial request, you would continue with the persuasive statement. "John, I know you've had a long day, but can you imagine how relieved you'll be when you walk in tomorrow and the report's complete?".

In this instance, although John is tired at the end of a busy workday, subliminal psychology triggers will quickly alert his senses. John will subconsciously feel respect and gratitude from you.

This makes it almost feel as though he needs to reciprocate the gratitude by accepting your request.

This subliminal psychology technique works so well because you're tapping into John's emotions to illustrate a pleasing scene. Once John is aware, he is in control of his ability to attain a state of pleasure, his mind begins wanting it.

By using his name to demonstrate respect and recognition, you've magnified your persuasiveness and ability to attain the desired result using a powerful subliminal psychology technique.

CHAPTER 6
HOW TO DETECT DECEPTION

Many people think they know how to spot deception. They rely on nonverbal signs or behavior which often speak louder than words. In reality, there are signs in the body language that can help decide if a person is telling the true story.

It's often thought that by looking at his eyes, you can tell if the person is honest. He is presumed honest if he looks straight in the eye. There have been instances, though, where nonverbal indications alone have failed to detect deception.

Lying, work suggests, is a talent. It's something you can learn—much like cycling, swimming, and driving. Professional liars have trained themselves to tell lies with a straight face, and after long hours of practice, they can do it with ease. Training talent involves the only discipline. If you want to learn how to spot deceit, it's best to use other resources than interpreting only body language signals.

Relying on nonverbal signs alone will contribute to misinterpretation. For some people, it can be quite stressful. This is especially valid when it comes to delicate and painful matters. For some, sexuality discussions are so uncomfortable that they cannot talk casually about it or look straight in the eye.

People continue to overestimate their abilities to spot deceit with false nonverbal signals so that they end up being fooled.

The method of detecting lies is very difficult because people rely on technical instruments to discover the facts. This objective approach might achieve a better rate of success than simply relying on nonverbal indications.

Lie identification devices are used under the statute in the interrogation of witnesses or suspects in crimes. These instruments demonstrate how incompetent the judgment of a human when it comes to interpreting signals is.

The polygraph and the functional magnetic resonance imaging, otherwise called FMRI, are some of the most common instruments used to uncover deceptions.

The polygraph checks and tracks the heart rate, skin conductance, and blood pressure of a person. Changes in the data being monitored are associated with anxiety levels for a person. During interrogation, when a person is anxious, there is a huge possibility that he lies.

FMRI is another technical tool that works for the same reason. It uses brain scans to understand how the mind of a person works and contains indicators that determine if a person tells the truth.

Service officers are learning how to spot fraud. They start the process by asking questions that are not threatening. These questions aren't prompting someone to lie. We then continue with the standardized interviewing process. They compare and observe changes in activity in the brain.

Again, sometimes these tools aren't exactly one hundred percent. Any normal person subject to a lie detector test, will trigger an increase in anxiety level and brain activity.

It can lead to misinterpretation of the data leading to the inference that even though he tells the truth, the individual is lying. He's just self-conscious or perhaps apprehensive of the computer!

This will pivot both directions. Professional liars can disguise their anxiety feelings, while others get stressed out by telling the truth!

Citizens do not, though, wring their hands and give up on those devices. We appear to forget that most of the people we associate with aren't trained liars, so not any of them are out there to cheat.

Operating with such a pessimistic attitude of their context will only draw more of such undesirable individuals. Let us be glad that science has come up with some instruments that can help to diagnose deceit in learning and understanding how it works.

CHAPTER 7
NLP TRAINING

NLP training and learning has two main areas of application: how we communicate with others and how we communicate with ourselves...

With NLP training, we learn to establish rapport (attunement) with most people, by becoming flexible in communication and using language (verbal and non-verbal or body) effectively.

We learn to deal with conflicts and solve them by learning to focus on solutions... NLP focuses on solutions, not problems.

Even with some NLP techniques, we can work with the internal conflicts that sometimes keep us in a state of indecision and internal division, especially when there are two internal parties with opposite interests.

We learn with Neurolinguistic Programming to discover and use our internal resources (trust, security, competence, inner peace, motivation, health, abundance, etc.), to discover our strategies (of excellence, creativity, good memory, etc.), to work with our beliefs and other levels of growth and learning. We become more aware of how our brains read, decipher, and encode our own experience, which is subjective.

Anyone who wants to improve their lives and develop understanding and awareness of how to develop and increase their potential can benefit from Neuro-Linguistic Programming.

Furthermore, anyone who wants to explore new tools and communication models can benefit from NLP's practice.

It's about cheering up, being curious and wanting to experiment... as NLP proposes ... you have to know that the reward is very great: greater understanding, emotional freedom, in short, a better quality of life!

Is NLP manipulation?

The discussion about NLP and manipulation is as old as the model. But this question is an important one for beginners.

Anyone who says to an NLPler as an inexperienced person that he has heard that NLP is manipulation will probably hear one of the following counter-arguments: With NLP, it is like a sharp knife: you can use it to cut bread or to violate someone. Ultimately, it is not the model that is manipulative, but the person. Correct. But not always convincing.

You will also hear: Every communication is

manipulation because, with every verbal or non-verbal statement, you influence other people. At this point, the well-known communication scientist and psychologist Paul Watzlawick with his much-quoted sentence, "You cannot communicate," is often consulted and quickly added: "And because every communication is influencing, you cannot manipulate either!". Not correct. Because influencing and manipulation are not synonyms. Therefore, this argument usually does not draw but leaves a stale aftertaste.

I can do a lot with the psychological-scientific definition of manipulation. It gives me a guideline on how to avoid manipulation as a person, because the potential for manipulation is undoubtedly there in NLP due to its high effectiveness.

In psychology, one speaks of manipulation if the following criteria are met:

1) Conscious influencing
2) For one's benefit
3) Accepting the disadvantage of the other

Point 1: "Conscious influencing."

We can answer "yes" in most cases where we use NLP. We want to influence with NLP—others and, of course, also ourselves.

Point 2: "For your benefit."

I would say very context-specifically. Sometimes yes (if I work on myself or if I want to build a good relationship with NLP techniques, for example, in an application and acquisition interview), sometimes also no (e.g., in coaching, if my client is the focus and my only concern is his Development).

Point 3: "Accept the disadvantage of the other"

Whenever I use an effective instrument to ensure that the other has a disadvantage or I accept a possible disadvantage, this does not correspond to NLP's ethical values. At least if we want to agree that conscious action to the detriment of another is generally not ethically justifiable.

For example, if I specifically build a good relationship with NLP techniques to encourage my counterpart to sign, which he doesn't want to do, then NLP is used in a manipulative manner. A good time to take a new path in which my counterpart can also have an advantage.

In the script of an NLP training institute, I even read the sentence in the context, "Is NLP manipulative?": "And yes, of course: NLP is effective because it is also lovingly and creatively manipulative. Some people have to be forced to their happiness or at least outwitted;" I do not agree with this, because what I consider happiness is only in my model of the world. How would I get to want to force my version of happiness on someone else?

How Quickly Can I Learn NLP?

The change can be something simple, or it can be something complex. It can occur gradually, exponentially, and sometimes unexpectedly. There are many and very diverse factors involved in this, and there is no single exchange rate. Based on this, there are many and different ways of creating and managing them, and many theories about it and its management.

Thus, change and learning are directly related. Depending on the type of result that you want to obtain and the situation that you want to improve, it may be appropriate to carry out a series of learnings that as a final result lead to a change or make a more direct change and that as a result of this are carried out a series of learnings.

To focus this writing, we will focus on a type of change and a type of learning associated with it and how NLP can help us carry them out. As always, we refer to changes in the personal and professional sphere, but in no case do we refer to the therapeutic sphere, since it is not within our sphere of action.

We focus, then, on a type of learning focused on the

acquisition and development of skills, and specifically on those in which we have to learn parts of what we want to know to finally put them together; which leads us to learn with a synergistic effect, in which the final result is greater than the simple sum of these parts separately. Taking the analogy of the practice of surfing, first, we learn to move the upper limbs, then the lower ones, later, putting them together, we learn to swim on the board; later, to stand up and, little by little, we are introducing new learnings until finally, possibly after falling many times and drinking a few liters of seawater, we can start catching the odd wave. What we have left in the end is a result of that.

This kind of change, in a predictable way, occurs with each new skill learned and incorporated into the previous ones; we are walking towards a greater change, and the sum of all of them leads us to a higher capacity.

Each of us has his way of learning, as well as his own time to digest each lived experience. It is in this framework, in that of learning, rather in the "how," we learn where NLP can contribute interesting principles.

It is where Neurolinguistic Programming (NLP) is very useful because it offers a range of resources that can facilitate this process of learning. Not only by speeding up the process but by ensuring that learning is done effectively.

How can NLP help

Three concepts can help you:

The language

In the process of change that we have mentioned, if it is about learning communication skills associated with the use of language (for example, improving communication with the team, learning to speak in public, developing active listening or creating harmony with the environment), NLP is very effective. This is because it has its own very complete and effective linguistic patterns, such as the metamodel, and the patterns of word ability. It also takes into account the entire communication process, attending and caring, in addition to language, all the non-verbal and para verbal elements present in communication, as well as the experience of communicating.

Furthermore, one of the important aspects of NLP, implicit in its name, is linguistics, directly related to what in NLP is often called linguistic representation. This is a process by which we assign meaning (linguistic label) to the information we receive from abroad in the form of images, sounds, sensations, touch, smells, tastes ... through a prior filtering process. Both (filtering and linguistic representation) are directly related to the act of communicating.

The effective use of this knowledge can be very effective when our learning is related to the improvement or development of communication skills. And it has a direct relationship with this type of learning, in which we acquire skills, as small parts that we add, until we reach a skill greater than the sum of these parts. This leads to a change, in this case, related with our communication.

Know the learning process itself

NLP offers you many resources to inquire into self-knowledge and understand how you shape your models. Among them, we have already spoken on this label, perceptual representations, submodalities, access codes, and long etcetera directly related to the learning experience.

Taking these aspects into account, adjusting them to each of those small learnings that we refer to in this type of change can make the learning and change experience more effective. To emphasize that we are always referring to this specific type of change and form the framework of NLP, and not to other types of learning and change, and the infinity of theories and ways of learning, we have maximum respect.

The core of NLP: Modeling

To speak of NLP is to speak of modeling. As in many currents, more emphasis is often placed on techniques (what we call patterns in NLP) than on the principles on which they are based. This possibly occurs due to its enormous versatility, practicality, effectiveness, and easy application. If we make an analogy with a complex process such as cooking, the techniques would be like knowing how to prepare a meal following the recipe. But knowing how the elements work (fire, water etc.) and the principles of raw materials is what allows us to develop recipes. Being able to cook without them, adapting to the circumstances the result of mixing the ingredients, that is, Modeling. Of course, the techniques are important, but if we know where they come from, we will be more effective, efficient, and flexible in putting them into practice.

To understand this concept, we must go back to its origin. You already know that Neurolinguistic Programming is born from the research work carried out by John Grinder, psychologist and linguist, and Richard Bandler, a computer scientist and psychologist, who, fascinated by studying human excellence, observed how three geniuses of the time did what they did: Fritz Perls (founder of Gestalt Therapy), Milton H. Erickson (expert hepatologist) and Virginia Satir (mother of Family Therapy). The purpose of the observation was to determine and make explicit the present distinctions of these people with a result well above the average in a specific field of action; that is, they modeled the patterns of cognitive, linguistic, and behavioral excellence of these three geniuses in the field.

But what is modeling? In close words, we can say that it is a very advanced and sophisticated way of learning and identifying the differences that underlie these results and that make the difference. What we call "the difference that makes the difference," that is, what causes a person to achieve an above-average result in a given field. And it is important to highlight this; that is, it is what makes you have an above-average result in a specific action in a given field.

And how can this serve in the learning processes associated with a change?

If the gradual learning that constitutes change is from language skills, skills related to the way we process information, or skills related to the way we behave, NLP, more specifically, NLP modeling facilitates a very concrete and advanced way of learning them.

Sometimes NLP modeling is confused with imitating or copying ... but in reality, it has nothing to do with that. NLP modeling is the essence of this advanced communication and change technology. It is thanks to this that it was created, and thanks to its new patterns (techniques) are developed, which makes NLP in constant evolution.

Modeling is not exclusive to NLP, but here we are talking about a very specific type of modeling. We will not go into more detail at the moment, give these brushstrokes of something that is very often left out, and that, however, is important to take into account when we talk about NLP.

Can you imagine if you could figure out and understand how you learn what you learn? What if you could learn about how you do what you do when you have a result in a specific performance? Don't you think that knowing it would be of value to your learning in the future?

To finish, a little reflection:

Throughout our lives, we have mastered skills that, at the time, we never even imagined; now, in the distance, it seems unimaginable not to have them.

Who would have told you that you would tie your shoelaces almost without looking or paying attention to each of the steps, right?

CHAPTER 8
MANIPULATE THE MIND THROUGH DARK NLP

Methods of Neuro-linguistic Programming

The neuro-linguistic programming methods are the specific techniques used to perform and teach neuro-linguistics. This pseudoscience teaches that people are not able to directly collect a small part of the world using their conscience; this point of view of the world is filtered by experience, beliefs, values, assumptions, and biological sensory systems. NLP maintains that people act and feel according to their perception of the world and how they feel about this world they subjectively live in.

NLP explains that vocabulary and actions (whether functional or dysfunctional) are rather organized and can be reproducibly "modelled" or replicated. Through NLP, a person will "create" the more effective aspects of their actions and reproduce it in situations where they are not successful. Or "model" another person and make adjustments in attitudes and habits to enhance the process. When someone excels at a task, we will understand how to do so exactly by looking at the essential aspects of their behavior. NLP embraces many methods, including hypnotic therapies that say proponents can induce improvements in thought, learning, and communication. NLP is a diverse area often described as a "toolbox" that has borrowed a lot from other fields, to collate its assumptions and techniques.

NLP considers each individual's view of the world their "map." NLP teaches that our mind-body (neuro) and what we say (language) combine to shape our views of the environment, or maps (programming). Each person's map in the universe dictates emotions and behaviors. Poor-and unrealistic-cards can, therefore, narrow choices and lead to problems. As an approach or therapy to personal development, it involves understanding that people create their own internal or world "map," recognizing unnecessary or destructive forms of thinking based on poor world maps, and then modifying or replacing these models with the most useful. "Modeling" in NLP is the practice of implementing another person's or model's actions, vocabulary, techniques, and values to "construct a model of what they do ... we realize that our modeling is effective because we can consistently produce the same outcome as the action of the person we have modeled on." The model is then simplified to a pattern that can be demonstrated to others. "Einspruch & Forman 1985 stipulates that" the modeler suspends his own beliefs when modeling another person and adopts the physiology, language, strategies, and belief structure of the person being modeled. Since the modeler will replicate the behaviors (speech, and behavioral outcomes) of the model behaviorally, a process happens in which the modeler modifies them and adopts his value system once again by incorporating the values of the model. "Modeling is not limited to education; it can and applies to a wide variety of human interaction. Another aspect of modeling is to consider the patterns of your actions to model the most productive aspects of you."

Milton model

The Milton model is a type of hypnotherapy based upon Milton Erickson 's linguistic models, a noted hypnotherapist, for hypnotic communication. It was described as "a way to use language to induce and maintain trance to contact our personality's hidden resources." The Milton model has three main aspects: first, to help build and maintain customer relations. Second, the conscious mind becomes overwhelmed and disturbed so that that implicit coordination can be established. Fourth, to enable understanding of the client 's provided terms.

1. Report

The first aspect, building relationships, or empathy, is done to achieve better communication and responsiveness. NLP teaches "mirroring" or the corresponding body language, posture, breathing, predicates, and voice tone. The report is an aspect of "stimulation" or development in the client or the world of learners. Once the rhythm is set, the practitioner can "lead" by changing their behavior or the perception that the other is following. O'Connor & Seymour's "Presentation of NLP" describes the report as a "harmonious dance," an extension of natural skills, but warn against mimicry.

2. Overload conscious attention

The Milton model's second characteristic is that it makes use of ambiguity in vocabulary and nonverbal contact. It can also be combined with vagueness, which arises when the limits of meaning are indistinct. The use of ambiguity and imprecision distracts the conscious mind from trying to understand what is meant, which allows the unconscious mind to thrive.

3. Indirect communication

The third feature of Milton's philosophy is that exposure to the unconscious is intentionally ambiguous and metaphorical. It is used to soften the meta-model and make indirect suggestions. A direct suggestion simply states what you wanted, for example, "when you are in front of the audience, you will not feel nervous." An indirect recommendation, on the other hand, is less hierarchical and leaves space for understanding. For example, "When you're in front of the crowd, you may become increasingly relaxed. This example follows the indirect method, both leaving the specific time and the level of self-confidence unspecified. It could be even more indirect by saying, "When you decide to speak in public, you can figure out how to know your feelings have changed." The choice of speaking to the public, the exact time, and likely responses to the whole process are framed, but the imprecise language gives the client the ability to fill in the finer details.

Representation systems

The idea that sensory systems or representational systems treat experience was incorporated into NLP psychology and gestalt therapy shortly after its creation. This helps us to view the world through the senses and to bear in mind knowledge from the senses. Memories are closely linked to the sensory experience. When people process the information, they see images and hear sounds and voices and process this with feelings created internally. Some representations are conscious, but the information is largely processed at the level of the unconscious. When they are involved in all tasks, such as talking, describing a problem in treatment, reading, then images, sounds, feelings (and perhaps smell and taste) are being activated at the same time. Furthermore, the systems are organized in a representative manner and the links between the repercussions on behavioral performance. Many NLP techniques rely on interrupting maladaptive models and replacing them with more positive and creative thinking models, which in turn impact behavior.

Preferred systems of representation

Originally, NLP taught that most people had a preferred internal representation system (PRS) and preferred to process information mainly in a sensory mode. The practitioner can determine this from external clues such as the direction of eye movements, posture, breathing, tone of voice, and use of sensory-based predicates. If a person repeatedly used predicates like "I can see a bright future for me," the words "see" and "brilliant" would be considered as visual predicates. On the contrary: "I feel that we will be comfortable" would be considered mainly kinaesthetic because of the predicates "feel" and "comfortable." These verbal cues could also be associated with changes in posture, skin color, or breathing changes. The idea was that the practitioner suited and operated within chosen structure of representation, could achieve better communication with the client and, therefore, faster and more effective results. Many training and standard works still teach PRS. At the same time, other promoters have de-emphasized the existence and relevance of the PRS and the workplace within putting the focus on all representation systems. Direct response to the sensory experience requires immediacy that respects the importance of the context. Grinder stated that the diagnosis of the representation system takes approximately 30 seconds.

Although some research supports the idea that eye movements can indicate visual and auditory (but not kinesthetic) elements of thought at that time, the existence of a valid preferred representation system of external signals (an important part of the original NLP theory) was updated by research in the 1980s.

Submodalities

Submodalities are the fine details of representation systems. In the 1970s, NLP developers began to play with the submodalities of representation systems involving the improvement of visualization techniques (common in sports psychology and meditation), including other sensory systems. Submodalities involve the size, location, brightness of internal images, volume and direction of internal voices and sounds, and the location, texture, and movement of sensations created internally.

Submodalities and hypnosis became the focus of further work by Richard Bandler. A typical change process may involve manipulation of the internal representation sub-modalities. For instance, someone may see their future as "dark and gloomy" with the accompanying emotions, but will try to interpret and experience as "bright and clear" by NLP.

Other training activities improve the capacity of an individual to transfer internal images, change the quality of sounds, and determine how these affect the intensity of feelings or other submodalities. Although NLP has not discovered submodalities, it appears that supporters of NLP may have been the first to systematically use manipulation of submodalities for therapeutic or personal development purposes, particularly phobias, compulsions, and the outbuildings.

Meta-programs

Neuro-Linguistic Programming (NLP) uses the term "meta-programs" specifically to indicate the general, pervasive, and frequent trends used by an individual in a wide range of situations. Examples of NLP meta-programs include a preference for insight or detail, preference for where to focus in conversation, usual language habits and body language, and so on.

Concepts associated with other disciplines are called cognitive styles or thinking styles.

In NLP, the term programs are used as a synonym for strategy, which are specific sequences of mental stages, most of the time indicated by their representational activity (using VAKOG), leading to a behavioral outcome. In the entry of the term strategy in their Encyclopedia, Robert Dilts and Judith Delozier explicitly refer to the mind as a metaphor for the computer: "A strategy is like a computer program, it tells you what to do with the information that you get, and, like the computer program, a lot of different types of information can be processed using the same strategy. "Dilts and Delozier then define metaprograms in their encyclopedia as: "[programs] which guide and other direct processes of thought. More specifically, they define common or typical patterns in the strategies or styles of thinking of an individual, a group or culture."

The book "Words that Change Minds" by Shelle Rose Charvet documents 13 separate meta-program categories affecting workplace motivation and performance, commonly known as language and behavioral profile or "LAB Profile." It is based on Rodger Bailey and Ross Steward, who wanted to make meta-programs usable for people without NLP training.

Aphorisms / presuppositions

The number and part of the presuppositions' substance can vary depending on the division of NLP (different teachers or companies). Any of them include:

The meaning of a communication is the answer you receive (not the one you'd expect).

Life is a structural system.

Body and mind are part of the same mechanism and have shared power.

Regulation involves range.

All conduct is tailored to adaptation.

There's a constructive meaning behind these behaviors.

People are doing the best they can with the available choices.

The choice is better than the other option (and the way you make a choice is a flexibility).

Several examples are greater than one.

In the context given, the behavior needs to be measured and evaluated or changed as necessary.

People already have all the necessary resources to succeed.

Someone's actions (present) is the highest quality knowledge you can get.

NLP teaches that "anchor points" (of classical conditioning) are continually being made between what we see, hear and touch and our emotional state. When an individual is exposed to a single stimulus (sight, sound, or touch) in an emotional state, a connection is made between the emotion and the single stimulus. If the single stimulus happens again, then the emotional state is triggered. NLP teaches that anchors (such as a particular memory or state-associated key) can be created and triggered deliberately to help people access "resourceful" or other target states. Anchors, as part of Virginia Satir's "style," tend to have been introduced into NLP for family therapy.

Future rhythm

A technique to ask a person to envision that they would do something in the future and monitor their reactions. It is generally used to verify that a process of change has been successful (i.e., by observing body language when the person imagines that he is in a difficult situation before and after the intervention). If the language of the body is the same, then the intervention did not succeed. In the context of the future, future stimulation may be used for "embedded" change. This provides a person with the experience of coping with a problem favorably before they get into it. It is focused on imagination, where the mind is not meant to discern the difference between an actual and visualized situation. The theory is that in reality, after having visualized positively when the subject again collides with the situation, the experience will serve to visualize a model of how to behave, even if this experience is imagined. The mind is unable to differentiate imagination from reality; it recognizes vision as fact and allows the transition.

Rustling

The rustling pattern is a process that is designed to disrupt a thinking pattern from one that serves to lead to unwanted behavior to one that leads to the desired behavior. This involves visualizing a "tail" that leads to unwanted behavior, such as a smoking hand moving with a cigarette towards the face and reprogramming the "switch" mind to visualize the desired result as a healthy, energetic, and fit person.

Additional sound effects are often imagined to enhance the experience in addition to visualization. Swish is one technique involving submodality manipulation.

Crop

Another technique, "reframing" functions by "changing the way you perceive an event and thus changing the meaning. When the meaning changes, so will the responses and behaviors. Language cropping allows you to see the world differently, and that will change its meaning. Reframing is the foundation of the most imaginative ways of thought, jokes, myths, folklore, fairy tales." There are examples in children's literature. Pollyanna played the Happy game whenever she felt down in life, remembering the things she could do, and not worrying about the things she couldn't. Alice Mills also says that this happens in Hans Christian Andersen's story from the surprise of the ugly duckling, the beautiful creatures welcome and accept it; looking at his reflection, he sees that he too is a swan. Cropping is common to several therapies and was not original to NLP.

An example of reframing can be found in the "Six Steps to Cropping," which consists of distinguishing between the underlying intention and the behaviors that flow from it to achieve the intention through different behaviors and more success. It is based on the premise that there is a good purpose under all actions, but that the activities themselves can be negative or against certain means. NLP uses this step-by-step process to identify the intent and make choices to satisfy that intent.

Well-formed result

In NLP, there are several "settings" in which the desired state is considered to be achievable and the effect if it is reached. The customer must define a positive outcome for its use, be in the customer's power to obtain, retain the positive products of unwanted behavior, and produce a result suitable for all circumstances.

Ecology

This is a framework in which the desired result is checked against the consequences in the lives of customers and relationships from all angles.

Integration of parts

"Integrating parts" is based on the idea that different aspects of our conflict are due to different perceptions and beliefs. "Parts integration" is the process of integrating disparate aspects by identifying and negotiating with the different parties to resolve the internal conflict. The integration of the pieces seems to be on the model of the "parts" of family therapy and has similarities with ego-state therapy in psychoanalysis.

CHAPTER 9
WHAT IS EMOTIONAL MANIPULATION?

As the chaos generated by planetary ascent accelerates, many people are influenced by negative forces which they do not understand. Some of these negative forces come from their Unconscious and their Negative Ego, which have strengthened a life made up of negative habits and behaviors. When people feel insecure inside themselves, they will easily resort to controlling and manipulative behaviors. It is useful to educate yourself about this behavior to protect yourself and create the necessary healthy limits.

People who are in control will always assume that their needs, wants, and goals are more important than yours. No matter what you can do or your responsibilities, they claim that you need to focus on them and their problems, no matter what the cost may be.

Even if the smartest of them aren't going to say it directly, the use of emotional manipulation will show you exactly what they're trying to accomplish. Through emotional manipulation, a person in control will use the empathy and compassion of others. He's a type of emotional vampire. Control behaviors are found in injured personalities of people who have low self-esteem, and thoughts of fear. When these fears are not addressed and resolved, this need to control others can evolve into narcissistic behaviors and psychopaths. An important point to understand about control behaviors is that the need to exercise control over others leads to the perpetuation of forms of manipulation. Manipulation of others leads to different degrees of deception and lying.

What is emotional manipulation?

For starters, there are many reasons why people feel the need to control people, places, and things, as well as to manipulate others to meet their personal needs, wants, and wishes. We are going to bring to the surface the most common problems based on the injured ego with little self-esteem and, therefore, little autonomy.

The people in control will always use manipulation tactics. It can be subtle techniques or master manipulators like many narcissistic personalities. Manipulation refers to the idea of trying to influence or control someone else's behavior or actions indirectly. As human beings, our negative emotions often cloud our discernment in such a way that it is difficult to see the reality behind the hidden agendas or motivations in different forms of behavior. The controlling aspects of the complexity of perpetuating deception are linked to emotional manipulation, to lying techniques, and are sometimes very subtle and can easily be overlooked. Often bad habits have been taken up through a negative ego that we have not worked on, whose control behaviors are driven away by feelings of guilt, low self-esteem, fears, and unethical behavior.

MOTIVATION OF MANIPULATORS

What are the possible motivations of a manipulator?

- The need to put forward their own goals and personal gain no matter what it costs others.
- A strong need to reach feelings of acceptance, power, and superiority about others.
- A desire and need to feel in control of people and the environment.
- A desire to gain a sense of power over others to increase their perception of self-esteem and worth in the world they create.
- A childish need to get what they want, coming from a high idea of themselves and no control over their impulses.
- A need to free themselves from inner anxiety and fear by projecting obligations on others to complete personal needs.

- The boredom of his environment, the desire to be entertained, or preoccupied with dramas.

Cause of manipulation

Why do some people so easily resort to manipulation of the emotions?

When a human being has never been able to grow up with loving parents who value self-esteem and know how to set healthy boundaries, from childhood to adulthood, he will be easily manipulated by his pain. If someone is easily manipulated by their unhealed trauma, abuse, injury, and lack of self-love, that person will grow into a manipulative adult with an emotional (suffering) body injured and immature. Most individuals seem to be adults who experience serious emotional trauma and revert to very unstable juvenile emotional conditions. The severe emotional wounds create a disconnection between soul and spirit sentiments.

Generally speaking, the age at which the most unhealed traumas occur in childhood is the age at which adults return when this injury is triggered in adult life. When this injury is triggered, the person will most of the time project the need to manipulate others due to their pain to get what they want, rather than taking responsibility for this pain. Then we can observe a person acting like a little child who has a crisis to get what they want. All parents know what it is like to have a two-year-old child screaming: "To me! Give it to me!" This is one of the reasons why we see a lot of adults behaving like emotional children when they cannot control the environment to get what they want.

Most healthy people understand that pretending to act to feel a certain way, or to play with someone else's emotions, is not morally ethical. But some people are so preoccupied with what they want and have such a high idea of their importance that they are not aware of manipulating or deceiving others.

Worse, some people have severe psychological schisms that create personality disorders that make them manipulate for pleasure or fun. When dealing with narcissistic people and psychopaths, it is important to remember that they are masters in manipulation techniques and protect themselves against their antics. Set healthy boundaries and do not accept the emotional manipulations and dramas of other people, and make it a priority in your life, because they will claim what they say. It is important to be a loving, and caring human being, but not a rug that is manhandled by psychic vampirism, which is the direct result of emotional and psychological manipulation.

Many manipulation techniques are very intelligent, and we can be stunned by the layers of complex deception techniques. However, the more educated we are about this, the easier it is to be aware of this behavior in others and to get rid of it yourself. When we embark on the Krystic path, we must consciously stop using manipulation techniques and control behaviors over others. This will minimize the chance of using emotional manipulation repeatedly to vampirize energies or to control your feelings of empathy for others. We each have the right to defend our own space that belongs to us, and to have the capacity to exist without being used as a rug prey to the manipulation of others. The obscure controllers do not agree with this freedom and are the promoters of these manipulation techniques.

Common Handling Techniques

What are the most common manipulation techniques?

MENTIR: It is important to realize that people will often lie about things; this can be a "little lie" or be very ambiguous in what one says. They can exaggerate to give the wrong impression. This can go where you question your ability to remember facts and trust what the manipulator says even when it is a lie. When we are facing a master manipulator, it is useful to take notes or even record the conversation so that you immortalize what has been said, and make it available to others around you, so that there are witnesses of the event. It is important not to allow a manipulative or controlling person to have authoritarian power.

GUILT: Most of us know what it's like to be guilty for someone else; often, we learn this behavior early from a family member. However, many manipulators are gifted and cleverly feel guilty when a person is open at heart and compassionate. In general, this is like making you feel bad or sorry for something you have not done or for which you are not responsible. In the heart, in care, and giving to others, they must remember that their feelings and energies are also important. Often what you can give is not enough, so the manipulator will make you feel guilty to show you how bad you are because you didn't give him what he wanted when he wanted. I have often noticed that when I don't jump when someone tells me to jump, he'll use guilt with manipulation. It often happens in spiritual communities.

BE WAVING TO TALK: It is obvious that many manipulation techniques are sneaky and deceitful. The manipulator can communicate in confusing terms and in ways that are not clear, which are hard to follow or understand. They can be passive-aggressive or congregate with colleagues or friends, on a plan that is against you. In this case, try by all means to communicate in an open, transparent, and as honest manner as possible to everyone involved. This method of creating confusion and doubt takes place in the hidden whispers of gossip and triangulation; in general, manipulations such as this one are done behind the curtain or in the shade. Bring the facts to light and speak clearly and transparently, tell the manipulator to look elsewhere.

CLAIM TO WANT TO HELP: It is a big problem in all groups, communities, or organizations. It is undoubtedly a painful problem that we have faced in our community. Manipulators and bullies like to pretend to be useful even when it is not their real motivation. What they want is a feeling of control over something or having access to someone. There may be a desire for power, status, or personal goal that the person thinks they can achieve by claiming to be useful to someone else. Often these people create a lot of destruction and extra work on the pretext of being "useful." When the person/organization that is supposed to receive the help ends up with additional issues, the person uses guilt to say how undervalued and underestimated they are. Open communication and the assessment of qualifications and emotional maturity are a necessity in any organization that concerns a group.

NO RESPONSIBILITY: When we understand how manipulation works, we want to discern responsibility for the situation or the person. Manipulators will always blame others for their wrongdoing, bad behavior, or unhappiness. If they fall into narcissism, they may think they are perfect and beyond reproach. Ending the manipulative blame game is the key to preventing this kind of deception from taking hold. If someone starts blaming you or blaming you when you don't do something, don't be intimidated, tell the truth.

DOUBLE SPEECH: Manipulators like to take anything that has been said and turn it around or twist its meaning to use it against you. Often with manipulators who are good at the double talk, the conversation will be mixed with confused and ambiguous language that doesn't make sense. It is often a lot of words, without meaning or substance. Sometimes a part may make sense, but the rest of the conversation has no connection to what was said. Double talk is a lack of consistency; the person may appear intelligent by using certain words, but they are often either confused or trying to confuse others to prevent them from seeing the truth. You may have listened to this person to speak for an hour and have no idea what it is. It can also happen a lot in relationships with strong emotional ties, and it will destroy trust and intimacy between people.

PSYCHIC VAMPIRE: A psychic vampire is a person who drains the energies of others and can intentionally drain positive energy and happiness in the other. In the manipulation tactics used to make a generally happy person feel bad or take their energy, the vampire will use condescending and demeaning behaviors. They can use bullying and harassment to make the other person feel insecure or completely dependent on them. Generally, with these people, we feel that we have to take tweezers not to irritate this person, or to awaken their rage. You don't know what can trigger them at any moment. If you notice that energy is drained when a person enters the room, you should protect yourself and amplify your 12D shield.

TYPES OF EMOTIONAL MANIPULATION

10 TYPES OF EMOTIONAL MANIPULATION

1. The sacrifice

For sure, you met 'the victim' at least once in your life. You simply know that each time they open their mouths, it is them. "I'm just not good enough," "You no longer love me," "You 're so crude to me, I'm fragile, can't you see?".

These people in their lives are always insecure about something, and they never know what to do, no matter what happens. They aim to get your approval and make them pity you.

Okay, no explanation why they're not named 'victims.' They want you all to feel sorry for them and give you all the power to make them feel better again because they can't make themselves feel better.

With this type of person, you may feel overwhelmed and get into a lot of fights because of their constant changes in mood.

2. All Professional

These people drain you most because their constant needs are so strong that they somehow manage never to show their insecurities better than anyone else. But imagine how vulnerable and insecure a person must be in constantly comparing himself with you and trying to belittle you by telling you how much better he is than you.

How they are above you and you are not deserving of their time. These men are using their toxic personalities to rob others. They can fill you with their insecurities and constantly point them to you so you can see every little mistake you have made. Let those guys just run away!

3. The flirty sort

Okay, what you can do when it comes to these type of people is to enjoy them and to smile. They are giving so much away to others that they seem desperate.

Perhaps because they are? You sure have a friend who is a toxic person in a flirty way. Yeah, you know that person who has no boundaries. She'll flirt with any ex you've ever got, with your friend's man, or even your boyfriend. She has no boundaries.

She's going to try and ruin your friendship and make you feel uncomfortable without ever knowing it!

4. The self defence man

So, you did something wrong, and it hurt somebody. You acknowledge that immediately. But not this guy, because the blame is on everyone else but him.

They are never the ones whose fault is that something has been broken or that some project has not ended the way it should have. They're going to make you believe you're the one who messed it all up, and they're never going to be blamed on anything.

5. The rage exploded

Some friends were like that, but they never noticed the pattern. They always felt they were too clingy and the one to blame. But they did not, they never did. It's just that for whatever reason, they're upset at themselves for not reaching a certain target or anything like that.

Don't care about these people, though. They have anger management problems, and you shouldn't have to think about it. They're not mad at you. They're angry at themselves.

6. The ruthless liar

They are going to make up a story only to sound more interesting. They want you to like them, so they're not going to make an excuse for it because why would they? This is an innocent lie. But beware.

You are never going to know if they are telling the truth about an important matter. They may even say lies about you, claiming, "Well, you didn't say it that way," or, "Oh, I must have misunderstood you."

7. The weaker strong

You've also met people who try to play the victim in relationships only because they're the 'weaker' gender, making their mate act like they're always watching out for them only because they won't get upset.

Somehow you want them to feel better, but it doesn't work. They are nothing but a dumb cry baby.

8. The three-way triangle

Weird name, huh? I have no idea what else to call them. These are sweet to their target, exploiting innocent people just to earn their trust.

They want the respect and affection of all the people they can associate themselves with, and they take advantage of the fact that they just get to ask what's going on and just to talk. They do not have their own identity.

9. The aggressive

If you're not doing what they want you to do, they could hurt you. Or at least they are trying to. Their language is a mixture of words of cursing and intimidation where they can affect you.

Do not take them personally; just try to converse with them in a friendly way. If it doesn't work anymore, then just leave. It's not worth the effort.

10. The 'everything-in-one'

This is probably an exaggeration, but in this world, some people are multiple emotional manipulators, and we have not recognized them until now.

If you don't do what they want, they can be the weak victims who threaten to kill you. But this is a fascinating mix.

And now? Now you know what to look for in people to see if they are mental manipulators. They mask themselves very well occasionally but trust me, they will finally reveal their colors.

Just keep your distance from these people, and don't devote your time to them. You'll feel more drained than you've ever experienced before.

EMOTIONS ARE CONTAGIOUS

When a person smiles, everyone smiles. When someone is crying, so others are crying. Feelings are genuinely experienced, but the problem is, what triggers the emotion? Is it that someone else communicates an emotion that activates our emotional reaction, or we feel like it's dependent on the case.

Recently, at a funeral, the priest, and then another one spoke, but there was no passion in their voices or the rest of the people; every eye was empty, including the children. Then the son stood up to speak, crying without even saying a word (not that it mattered since he spoke English and most people couldn't). The bulk of people quickly started weeping as well. Also, I could sense swirling feelings, and I didn't have any relation to the deceased, I was filming the footage. That's awesome, her life has or didn't have anything to do with my career, nor would she have. Nothing has changed, nothing has been said, and in a moment a cool, calm audience has turned into a tearful crowd simply by someone who has the attention of everyone starting to cry.

Think of how many times laughter, tears or yawning had come when someone else did. So how can we call that emotion real, even if it's felt sincerely? If it were real, another person would not need to trigger it, it would come of its own, and that is a real emotion. Contagious thoughts are cerebral too.

That is why films and television shows have fake laughter. If the joke isn't funny, because laugher is contagious and some people laugh, the audience will laugh. The same with crying, one guy cries, then everyone is weeping; that's the best actor's skill.

It is as contagious as the common cold to cry because you cannot help the emotional feeling, even if your emotions are triggered by the actions of another person who may simply be a good actor.

When you're a very good, emotionally stable person, you're not going to be influenced by others' feelings, which might be meant to exploit you. The experts in charity promotion are good at that. The value of being emotionally stable and conscious that your feelings are most born in intelligence is important for you not to get swept up in the put-on feelings of a successful salesman or someone who causes your emotions to exploit you.

The theory that abstract reasoning forms the vast majority of our feelings is easy enough to prove. Whatever you feel, could you have felt that you identified and felt a certain way if you didn't get some information in your mind? For example, you'll feel an emotion if you get an email that your friend's father died and understand those words. Nevertheless, if the same details came in a letter in a language you couldn't understand, you could read the mail phonetically so you wouldn't feel any emotion. You have to process the information first, and then respond. When you received the email and heard it, you may feel depressed but then, minutes later, your friend called you up and was excited and hopeful about the death of the father, your feelings might also change.

The knowledge you receive is mentally analyzed, and depending on that, your feelings alter. I'm sure you will consider a lot of cases in your life or someone else. On the other hand, if you enter a very filthy public toilet in China or India that hasn't been washed in months and used by hundreds of thousands of people right away because the stench filled your senses, you will have a very simple, immediate, and pure reaction without intelligence. There's no need to think and analyze before you feel sick, nor is there even time to do so. If you get the gross feeling brought on by the odor and mental picture, you will see how solely rational your emotional response is, because you're definitely in a clean environment. The feelings are not real; they are constructions of thought.

Children show the vast majority of our emotions are not at all emotional, but purely intellectual. Children don't respond when a child falls and it's a really serious injury; children look at the adult first, then wait for the parent's response. If the parent jumps up and says, "Woooooooooh!" There, we see how the mind and emotions function and turn us into the extremely reactive or very resilient person we are.

It shows how feelings aren't genuine and are instead infectious and intelligent. The value of this is freeing oneself from the emotional swings that control our lives. Many people lead tragic lives when their feelings are out of control; they are very dependent on emotion. They focus on feelings or things so they can recognize and care about, generating sensations that they can experience. We cause conflicts or tragedies while life is peaceful, or associate with otherwise straightforward and benign events, turning them into earth-shattering issues.

We can see this in people who struggle vehemently over topics that have no relevance to their lives or anyone else, things that are just normal and part of the world, and will pass unless you deliberately put yourself on the train path. How many times have you met someone happy or upset over something you considered trivial? And when you wanted to figure out why they felt this way, there was no other logical explanation except, "because that guy told me to get over it, so he was enthusiastic about it."

A large portion of our days is wasted or lost in emotional experiences that are often pessimistic and upsetting. An occurrence happens, it is typically small, but we make it significant in our heads and have a proportional emotional reaction. Not only is the feeling heightened, but the time it lives on. Most people keep an experience alive and feel profoundly good for years after it's gone by, and nobody else remembers it. They can tend to feel very depressed, emotionally. Yet it's just their emotional work that keeps them feeling alive and ever-growing when they're sad. If anything happens, just at a really good moment, the mood shifts. When you had immense love for someone, and it was pure feeling, even though you had a car crash or a lot of tension at work, the affection for that person would always be high, very irrelevant to the situation at hand. This is the difference between a true and an abstract feeling.

The great mark of a snake-oil salesman is to convey self-praising thoughts that trigger emotions in the audience, so they buy his products or join the flock of sheep by feeling great positive emotions in his presence when they later think of him. That is the trick that makes people victims, without realizing it, to emotional coercion. They begin fooled into thinking, and of course, they are asked to believe their emotions.

The feelings are really strong, but true and rational are two types. Once you know the difference and stop succumbing to the rational impulses, you will have absolute strength and influence of your life.

WHY ARE THEY SO IMPORTANT TO SALESMEN?

We've been influenced by the selling giants of the past few years that we now know as sales gurus. They have achieved greatness using traditional sales techniques, and these techniques have been our reference points. The truth, though, is that deceptive methods derive their inspiration from conventional sales techniques.

Next, it is imperative to know what the methods of emotional manipulation are. Second, by being aware of them, it is also important to avoid them, because it is a felony to use manipulative techniques to win over prospects.

Traditional vs. New Approach to Marketing

There has been a lot of change in consumer purchase behavior due to globalization, so that consumers add value to the relationship. Potential consumers choose to buy products for present and potential use, and instead manipulators behave as if they lack the common theory. Therefore, the fear of selling alone binds salespeople to both conventional and new closing strategies. And the challenging part here is whether to use the two sales methods or prefer one over the other. Not all conventional selling strategies are to drop, but the main element is self-willingness to distinguish what is required.

It's fraud

Compared to various interpretations, deception is the act of playing with someone's feelings in order to gain self-interest. Is it really appropriate to exploit the minds of customers by making them think things like, "This is the last day of sales?" Is this the only way to settle a deal? However, playing with the mind of a future buyer to generate anxiety by using these methods has become outdated. Clients have modified their way of developing standards, so it is now time for salespeople to adapt approaches to this new ideology.

The selling adventure playground is paired with a range of potential buyers with specific desires. The truth is that each reacts differently, so it is up to the salesperson's desire to determine what the terms of the deal are. And by employing a misleading tactic to market, we have to keep in mind that the facts will inevitably come revealed in one direction or another. Remember, the main goal is not simply to sell, but to generate repeat purchases from the same customer.

How to connect and stop being fooled during transactions

Persuasiveness

Persuasion is permitted in transactions, but the intent behind it is what matters. Asking a valid question should not be exploited but maximized to consider that we are able to offer alternatives to customers. Nevertheless, a different meaning than that is called deceptive. Ethical selling activities are internally guided, not externally inspired. When you believe your strategy would help your client and the profit margin of your business, why would you apply manipulation?

Therefore, a selling technique focused on deception is a harmful tool against the drug solution or business. And any slight mistake, the impact is going to be huge and impossible to catch up with. Intents with the goal of compelling self-benefit prospects should be resisted by all means. Sales techniques, however, should therefore be consistent with current sales practices.

Five Ways to Save You from Emotional Manipulators

Mental manipulators and techniques that they use to manipulate you is worth learning about. The destruction that these emotional predators will inflict in your life is sinister and dangerous. Such people will wear you down until you're a sad, vanquished shell of the person you once were. That's why it's necessary to understand the strategies they use to conquer and set strict boundaries to defend yourself from them.

Note, the emotional manipulator (EM) cannot be modified. But you can adjust the way that you react to them. When you know the methods that they employ, you will be prepared to adjust your actions and defend yourself from violence.

1) Stand up for yourself, please. If the EM brings you down and makes you feel lost or powerless, fight back. Don't let them get away with this stuff. Below is an example of an emotional manipulator attempting to make you feel bad. EM is doing a job, say, washing the cat litter. Here is the conversation:

- You: Let me help you do that.
- EM: No, I've got that.
- You: Okay, okay.
- EM: (Cat Room Cleaning) Sigh.

You're not saying a word. You have offered; the EM has declined your support. Now the EM is making sighs and sounds of frustration, as you thought she was going to do. She's actually finishing the job.

- EM: It would have been great to have some help with that.
- You: I offered it, but you refused.
- EM: You don't know how to clean a cat box properly.
- You: I do, of course. You know that just as well as I do.

The trick is to stand up for yourself and refuse to embrace the EM gambit. When an emotional manipulator discovers a tactic that works on you, you're lost. They're going to press that on you again and again.

2) Set clear limits. This is sometimes complicated, because the emotional manipulator can be so devious that you don't even grasp all their tactics. Start by having a talk with the EM about what you can no longer tolerate. Acknowledge that you've been up against the actions of the EM in the past, but you won't tolerate the violence any longer. Tell the EM that you want them to stop calling a name, use sarcasm to bring you down, raise their voice to scream at you, swear a blue streak, threaten your appearance, or some other actions you find disconcerting.

3) Create strong implications. If an EM crosses the barriers you've set—and they're likely to—they will know there's going to be repercussions. Tell them you're not going to communicate with them anymore. You're leaving the place. Then you do it. Go somewhere else, listen to the radio. Have a bath. Wear the headphones so you can't hear them. Well, whatever it takes. Be willing to do this over and over again before the action of the EM changes. You're going to have to stand your ground and never give in.

And don't bluff it out. Establish only certain effects that you are prepared to carry out.

4) Believe your intuition. When the EM is trying to get you to do their dirty work, particularly if it makes you feel awkward, listen to yourself. If you don't want to do so, even if they feel unable to do it on their own, decline respectfully. They could even say things like, "I have every faith that you will do something on your own." Take choices that are good for you, not for the EM. A lot of EM's will suck the life out of a room and you. Resist it. Look for positive feelings and what feels good to you.

5) Know when you should call it quits. Relationships can't be rescued often. EM's are emotionally weak and need to torture and dominate you to feel emotionally safe and fulfilled. EM's need help, but they never understand that. If you're in a relationship with an EM, you can try to get help for them, but don't be disappointed if they hesitate. You might also benefit from therapy. But at the end of the day, you may have to end the relationship.

ENLIGHTENMENT OR EMOTIONAL INDEPENDENCE

Of course, the most appealing is salvation, spiritual awareness, self-knowledge, or something in that direction.

What I think is more important to reflect on is the equality of the emotions. The Sufi and the Kabbalists say, "Freedom is not about what anyone thinks or says about you."

This state of being is a life in which you can never be insulted, hurt, or manipulated emotionally. Anger and conflicts rarely occur with those emotional buttons removed from your life, yet joyful events increase.

No one can attain significant spiritual growth or enlightenment without emotional freedom, also known as equanimity or a stoic character.

Thus the best path is one that seeks emotional freedom not only because it is a prerequisite for spiritual growth but because it is very difficult to achieve enlightenment, and a life spent in that pursuit may not change much. However, emotional equality is fairly easy to obtain, and will certainly and significantly enhance the quality of life for everyone.

In this chapter, I'll present a very brief outline of the theory.

Knowing that you never really understand what the other person means in words they utter is the fundamental concept for attaining equality.

You can't get upset or hurt because you understand. How do you get emotional conflict if you agree? And when you understand, how can you disagree? So we can safely say that any conflict or negative emotion is based on an incomprehension.

The goal is to be able to understand in the deepest possible way. This is the aim of our work, to remove the blocks that prevent us from really understanding another person or the situation.

Understanding and then agreeing doesn't mean you are losing your values or giving up all your beliefs. Rather it means you see things from the viewpoint of the other guy. At the same time, we can quickly see things from different perspectives. When we don't understand, we often think we understand the other person and disagree. Your emotional reaction is the test. Any negative in any way means that you have not really understood it, but rather have taken it personally in your subjective interpretation.

The point is that if you see it from the other person's point of view, or understand what they mean instead of taking your interpretation of what they were saying to be what they meant, then you can understand it and therefore, cannot be upset because you are in harmony. When we are in equilibrium, we cannot have a negative emotion.

Once in harmony, free from negativity, including anger, conflict, self-pity, self-attack, and a host of other negative emotions, we can calmly express our opinion. On the other hand, you may find your opinion incorrect or unnecessary and drop it entirely. Or you can find this one moment in peace, and the other person will be more receptive to hearing what you think so you can describe it in a way they understand.

Our life is all about our opinions. We have opinions about everything, even what some words mean or what a person means when he says certain things. The problem is that those views are highly subjective. They are yours and don't often match up with others.

The principle of working is to open the mind, become truly objective, and remove the self-limiting fixed opinions, among other positive changes of our being.

If you achieve nothing else in life than being impervious to any emotional attack or manipulation, free from anger and conflict, you will have achieved much. Imagine how much good you can do in the world, with these qualities? If everybody knew each other and lived in peace, what will the world be like?

It's so easy to achieve if we can concentrate our lives on goals that are realistic and feasible instead of striving for goals that we can't accomplish because we didn't train our minds to hit that point.

One single step at a time. First, master human beings, then work to be more than just another human being.

EMOTIONAL VULNERABILITY IS NOT LIFE-THREATENING

(Unprotected) Vulnerable: open to physical injury or attack; capable of being injured or wounded.

How do we NOT fear to expose ourselves? Our insecurities, our shortcomings, our skeletons in the closet, and those dirty little secrets. All those things make us uncomfortable talking about the way we truly feel. All of these things are connected to an emotion. Emotions are not life-threatening. The truth is that we are fearful of our own emotions. Our desire to feel positive emotions manipulates our actions.

FEAR is what holds us back from living and loving. Fear of being judged and being rejected while being vulnerable emotionally for speaking the truth about what is on our mind. Having to answer for something we "got away with" haunts our conscious mind so we protect it, hide it, and bury it away where nobody will ever discover the truth. The problem is; we know we seek to be accepted for what we are, and when we do not allow our true self to be vulnerable, we deny ourselves the opportunity to be accepted.

We all have the desire to be appreciated, accepted, loved, and admired. Fear of being emotionally vulnerable is self-sabotaging and prevents us from what we strive to achieve.

We've all heard it said, "The truth will set you free." Self-esteem and confidence are some of the rewards for those who risk rejection. The truth is when we "cheat" by not exposing our vulnerabilities, we lack courage. Courage is not a lack of fear; it is scary, and you still do the honorable thing. When you are honest with yourself and true to your conscious, take a stand even when the outcome is undetermined and unpredictable. The two possible outcomes are accepted or rejected. The butterflies in your stomach may feel like pterodactyls. Your mind may be screaming, and your heart may be crying. The emotions may feel like a tornado inside. Understand that what you are feeling is FEAR. You are feeling emotionally vulnerable and are fearful because, in your mind, someone is about to pass a verdict to accept or reject whatever it is that you are "standing for." Understand that it is not you they are accepting or rejecting; it is what you are standing for that they are deciding about.

I have had the misfortune of many hurt feelings, and I am still here to talk about it. I have experienced both acceptance and rejection. In everything I have ever done, some of the most terrifying and liberating things I have accomplished was having COURAGE. Courage will lead you down the path to greater self-esteem and confidence. You will attract people of like mind to you and whatever it is that you desire. With over 6 billion people on this ball of dirt we call Earth, do you believe you are alone?

Your true choice is to be the master of your fears or allow your fears to manipulate you. Emotional vulnerability is required to build courage. Courage is required to build confidence and self-esteem. With practice, you will start mastering your fears, but you will attract many wonderful and amazing people and things into your life.

You may find that your display of courage inspires others to be free from emotional bondage, and the many forms of depression that affect entire families. How would that boost your confidence and self-esteem?

Many people are depressed for avoidable reasons. I believe that FEAR is the largest contributor to the massive rise in people classified as clinically depressed. Medications may help people cope. I believe there is a cure. That cure starts with understanding that emotional vulnerability is an illusion. Nobody has ever died because someone hurt their feelings. Many people do, however, live in FEAR of the next panic attack.

Courage to accept your own emotions and instincts will prove to yourself that you have every right to be different and unique... just like everyone else.

When you don't show someone who you are and let that someone decide that you're "the one," you will never really know! (Self-sabotaging insecurity)

CHAPTER 10
BEHAVIORAL AND CHARACTER TRAITS OF MANIPULATORS

Manipulators: two main types of personality

To clarify things, I would first say that we are not all manipulators as some say. We all sometimes have a manipulative behavior, but it remains occasional and it does not have the color of destructiveness as is the case with the manipulator.

The narcissistic manipulator

The best known and best described is that of the narcissistic manipulator: he seeks power in his relationships and is recognized for his narcissistic seduction thanks to the attributes of power. He manifests in the early stages of the relationship an apparent sympathy, a search for common ground, a false understanding and protective attitude.

All of this is a calculation to initiate his grip relationship over the other. Then, the other must conform to whatever he wants and thinks, otherwise he is devalued, made to feel guilty, threatened ... He believes himself to be perfect and does not question himself, on the other hand he stigmatizes the other for their imperfections by playing on their moral values. He is in perpetual quest for admiration, recognition, but does not know how to love, because he does not recognize the other in his difference.

The perverse narcissistic manipulator

He differs from the previous one, because he is motivated by the desire for destruction of the other in his narcissism in order to inflate his own. He searches for the grip by the same game of seduction as the previous one, but once the grip is installed, he isolates and harasses his victim until he loses all his narcissistic energy, falls into depression, psychosomatic illness or until he commits suicide.

Harassment manifests itself in verbal and nonverbal violence: insults, devaluations, guilt, threats, blackmail, contempt, paradoxical language (words are contradicted by gestures, for example, or two sentences cancel each other out).

He makes the other angry with these attacks, and then blames them for that. On the outside, he seems sympathetic, moral, but alone in front of his victim, he is violent and seeks to destroy her, hence his perverse aspect.

He believes himself above the law and has no guilt, has no morals, no sense of forbidden and lies despite the evidence. He is in the denial of the other who can only be an undifferentiated part of himself, in the denial of his own suffering as that of the other. He never questions himself but can play comedy very well. He is empty internally, evolving only in intellect and calculation. He instrumentalizes the other who is for him only an object to exploit, then to throw away. When he has exhausted his prey, he chooses another. When the latter succeeds in fleeing, he immediately finds another.

The most effective techniques to use: Emotional

Managing Your Emotions Better: 10 Techniques That Work

Your emotions do not appear or disappear when you decide. But, can you have power over feelings, or do you have to surrender to them dominating your actions?

Do you ever wonder why someone would talk in public without being anxious when someone else is unable to do so? Why are there people who succumb to wrath in a debate while others stay calm?

While it's okay to feel sad when you hear bad news, it doesn't mean that your only option is to keep crying in a corner (this attitude probably keeps you upset for longer). Recognizing that you are sad while forcing yourself to do something productive will help you feel better ahead of time.

What happens when your emotions lose control?

You can't help but feel the feelings. Emotions are there because they have an intrinsic role, a psychological sense of survival. If our ancestors hadn't felt fear in front of a pack of lions, the human being probably wouldn't have lived to this day.

As if it were an automatic reaction in the form of violence or flight from a threat, the amygdala is the portion of the brain that is responsible for shooting emotions. That is why it is so hard to control the root of your emotions by force of will: it would mean canceling the response for which you are genetically programmed.

So, this kind of emotional response is required. It's not correctly adapted in certain men, however, so it can happen that they:

- Trigger in situations where there is no real threat (by causing anxiety)
- Are unable to deactivate them over time (as in the case of depression). For some reason, the

brain enters a mode of survival and remains anchored there.

When you are in a phase of struggle in the face of aggression or flight and the amygdala has taken control of your actions, normally it is already too late. This is why; you must learn to act beforehand. You have to get used to detecting these signals that tell you that you are going towards the path where you cannot dominate your emotions.

It's the only way you'll be able to stop the process (or delay it) before it's too late. Once emotions dominate you, you are little more than a beast that feels hunted down.

The Truth about Negative Emotions

The most recent theory is that there are 4 basic types of emotions that have evolved into the rest of the more complex feelings. These emotions are irritation, fear, joy and sadness.

There are a few situations that you can never get used to. If all goes wrong, you will hardly be able to leave behind the feeling of fear or anxiety. However, positive emotions are used to disappearing over time. Win money in the lottery or be so much in love: positive emotions like pleasure always end up diminishing.

In fact, in one study it was determined that the emotion that lasts the longest is sadness. In short, it even lasts 4 times longer than joy.

What doesn't work to control your emotions?

These techniques have become popular by word of mouth from authors who have not bothered to verify their actual scientific basis. The usefulness of each of them to process your emotions is, at least, questionable.

1. Try not to worry about your thoughts

Much as trying not to think about a white polar bear can cause you to end up thinking about it in a rebound effect, it has been shown in research that extracting the feelings from our brain is very difficult.

In the case of suicidal people continually attacked by negative thoughts, trying to eliminate these ideas is contraindicated as they end up coming back with far more intensity.

2. Relax and take a deep breath ...

It is normal to be advised to relax and breathe deeply when we are irritated or very nervous. This comes from an almost ancient tradition, like that of breathing inside a plastic bag in a panic attack.

There's one downside, though. Breathing deeply and attempting to modulate the diaphragm doesn't really work because the physiological aspect of the emotions typically doesn't matter.

In the majority of the occasions in which you were very annoyed, where, for example, you were quiet before becoming irascible, you probably had a good day until someone ruined it: am I wrong?

If a previous state of relaxation could not prevent you from being annoyed: why do people believe that they can get it once they are already angry?

Have you ever recommended that someone relax when they are annoyed? You will realize that generally ... it doesn't work very well. It is as if instead of listening to the one who suffered an injustice, you recommend him to be silent and take a tranquilizer.

With that I don't mean that using relaxation techniques is bad. Besides, meditating is quite useful. But trying to relax after the emotions overwhelm you is going to treat the symptom, not the cause.

3. Release the tension by other means

There was a time when activities to release emotions were in fashion. Workshops where people gathered to cry or events where aggressive executives broke plates.

Well, recent psychological studies suggest that this type of catharsis does not work. Even that it can be negative: succumbing to the temptation to tear everything apart can increase your aggressiveness in the short term. The same thing happens when you exercise: even if it is good for your heart, physical activity cannot calm your emotions.

Emotions are not contained inside our body and do not need to go out as if we were pressure cookers. What they need is to be understood to prevent them from harming us.

4. Forcing yourself to have positive thoughts

There is a bit of controversy over the effect of having optimistic thoughts about regulating emotions. Although I would not say that they are able to make you pass from a negative state to a positive, but they can manage to reduce the intensity of a negative emotion.

Emotions are processed almost in their entirety on an unconscious level and then move on to the conscious space, where you perceive them. This is why, when you become aware of your emotions, it is often already too late.

However, looking for the positive part of each situation can prevent you from continuing to sabotage yourself. If, instead of thinking "I'm not going to be able to do this," you start to believe "It's complicated, but I can control it," then you will prevent your negative emotions from getting worse.

Which is it?

True emotional intelligence allows you to make your own moods known and understood. It includes knowing when and why you are irritated, anxious or sad and acting on the causes, not just the symptoms.

Nonetheless, the following methods can be effective at halting or slowing this chain reaction on certain occasions when you see that you are irreparably heading for a destructive emotional state.

1. Try to remember your virtues and successes

Reaffirming your virtues and strengths is one of the best strategies for managing your feelings. It consists in thinking about what caused you this emotion but by reducing its negative meaning.

An example: Instead of being annoyed because you arrived late at work you can think that, since you always arrive on time, it is not so serious.

People with greater emotional control use self-affirmation when the intensity of their emotions is still low and they have time to seek another perspective on the situation. Curiously, it has been shown that this strategy works especially well in women.

The next time you feel that you are losing control over your emotions, remember the things you pride yourself on in your life.

2. Turn your attention away from something specific

People who control their emotions best have often learned to use diversion until it's always too late to avoid emotional states. Now, when they expect that they will feel strong and do not have enough time to use other methods, it seems very successful.

As you know, diverting his focus is a very effective way of soothing a little boy who keeps crying: "Have you seen the doll?" or: "What do I have in my hand?" If we hold their attention for long enough, it helps to increase their level of enthusiasm.

The strategy of diversion is to separate yourself from the negative emotion by shifting your focus to rational thoughts. In this type, you should prevent too much strength from obtaining in the emotion.

For example, if your boss challenges your integrity instead of thinking he's going to fire you, you might worry about the Saturday birthday party that you have. As a few scientific studies have shown, it's easy but successful.

Although it may not be the best long-term strategy, diversion works, particularly if you concentrate on something specific rather than letting your mind wander around.

3. Only think about the nearest future

Very strong feelings can make you forget that there's a future and that it's going to affect your actions. Though you're just thinking of living in the present moment and your anger at this moment, an annoyance where your nerves take on a lot of importance, are you going to continue to feel this for a whole week?

Thinking about the most immediate future is very effective in maintaining self-control, as has been demonstrated in the experience of the popular book Emotional Intelligence. In this book, children who have resisted the temptation to eat a treat have fared better in their schoolwork in future years.

4. Meditate daily

Meditation has scientifically demonstrated its effectiveness in preventing repetitive negative thoughts, not only while you meditate, but also in the long term: it can decrease the level of activation of the tonsil in the long term.

Meditation has also been the subject of studies for anxiety reduction. In one, four 20-minute meditation sessions were enough to reduce anxiety by 39%.

Trying to relax only when the emotions assail you is not very effective. However, meditating regularly and breathing properly can reduce the intensity of negative emotions when they arise.

5. Give yourself permission to worry later

Earlier, I explained to you that trying to suppress an emotion or a thought causes it to come back again with more force. However: adjourning it for later may work!

In one study, participants with anxious thoughts were asked to defer their concern for 30 minutes. Although this is an alternative form of avoiding thinking about something, what has been shown is that after a period of pause, the emotions return with much less intensity.

So give yourself permission to worry after this waiting time. You will care less.

6. Think of the worst that can happen to you

Do you remember the movie Unforgiving by Clint Eastwood?

In this film, the character William Munny, is the best hitman in the west despite the fact that he is old and there is no hope for him. And it's not for his speed or precision. As he himself says, it's because when the bullets start to fly, he controls his emotions and keeps calm.

But: how to maintain calm? The samurai and the stoics kept quiet even in the most dramatic situations: how did they get it? Thinking about death, and a lot.

I don't want you to get dramatic or turn into Gothic, but thinking about the worst that could happen to you will help put things into perspective and keep you in control.

7. Write your emotions in a journal

Expressive writing consists of writing on your deepest thoughts and feelings and it has proven to be effective both on a psychological and physical level (it is able to accelerate the healing of wounds!).

Keeping some kind of emotional journal about what you have felt in certain situations will help you reduce the recurrence of negative thoughts.

8. Take a deep breath and refresh to recover self-control

Your self-control is not infinite. Some research indicates that by exposing yourself to situations where you have to control yourself, this ability is consumed.

Think of it like sprinting. After the race you are exhausted and you need time to recover before starting to run again. In the same way, if you manage to control your emotions, avoid starting to expose yourself again to a tense situation or it will be more likely that you will succumb.

The most shocking thing is, as it has been proven that retaining power absorbs glucose, as though you were doing it literally. Therefore, you have two methods for regaining your self-control:

1. Take a drink rich in sugars (this is not a joke).
2. Use positive reaffirmation to be able to deal with your emotions again.

The key is in identifying when your levels of self-control are low and avoiding more emotional situations while you are recovering from strengths.

9. When nothing will work, look for a mirror

Sorry? To look in the mirror? Yes, even if it may seem very surprising, this strategy can be useful to stop you when you are too caught up in your emotions.

Some studies have shown that when you see yourself reflected, you are able to observe yourself from a more objective perspective and therefore separate yourself for a few moments from your emotions.

The more you are aware of what you are doing, the more capable you would be of controlling your emotions. Looking at yourself in a mirror will raise your self-awareness levels and help you act in a more friendly manner.

10. That's it. Most important: figure out the reason for your feelings

In the long run, the trick is not battling your feelings but understanding and knowing why they are happening to you. Use, for example:

"Okay, I don't like to talk like that, but right now, I just want (you know the emotion) because André has been congratulated for his work, and I don't (you understand why)."

The main thing is to be the same frank about the cause for the emotion with yourself.

Don't be like the majority in trying to make a mistake. We often lie to ourselves by making ourselves believe that we are annoyed by someone by their behaviour and not because they gave him the promotion to which we aspire and that affected our self-esteem.

CHAPTER 11
HOW TO USE MANIPULATION IN SEDUCTION

We manipulate you! Not us, no. But girls, guys, the media, politicians, your mother, your brother, your best friend, your boss, everyone manipulates everyone to simplify their lives.

We have prepared for you a selection of manipulation techniques... (and influence) to simplify your life. Some are adaptable to seduction, others a little less, but you will recognize all these situations that you have already experienced!

Let us agree: Manipulation is bad, like lying. Lying to get what you want at the expense of others is a shame. Influence is better: get more for yourself and others. Using your influence, as they say, is positive.

But then why talk about manipulation here? Not to make you manipulators, no, but indeed so that you can identify the people who are trying to trick you, or who are trying to take advantage of your friends.

Here are seven techniques that will make your life easier if you know them (and recognize them when they try to catch you).

Kind manipulation: Helping the other to wait for a return service.

It is called gaining credit. I can only encourage you to read the Essay on The Gift Of Marcel Mauss. It is one of the foundations of sociology and exchanges between humans.

From the moment you give someone a gift, you enter a process of donations and counter-donations that strengthens ties and develop communities (and peace).

The nice manipulator will give the girl a gift, do her a favor, do something good for her, and she will feel indebted a little, or a lot.

In reality, it's a terrible technique; it's really big manipulation because the girl puts her feet in a trap with no idea. An example is a potential client who prompts you to sign a contract... if you kiss him or if you accept a more "informal" dinner with him.

Request favors in public

Another manipulation technique derived from business. Once, during a meeting, I found myself trapped by a superior who wanted me to do his job. And I was an intern.

He knew very well that face to face, I would have told him that it was not my mission (I was a bit of a wanker for a time) and that I was not going to work for him. But faced with popular pressure, the looks of all those eyes around me, I was forced to say, "Yes, of course."

Trapped by social pressure, I swear... In seduction, it can also apply when a girl in the group requests a service, like someone to go to IKEA or to give her language lessons.

When you are the only one to propose yourself and the group says, "Well yes, go with him!" she cannot publicly say, "But no, he is too soft, too insistent, not my type, I do not want to go with him."

Another trap that closes and which big manipulators love. Ah, I have another example that comes to mind: the one where a girl wants to return home after a long evening at a nightclub with friends, and you are the only one who has a car to accompany her.

When you propose to bring her home and thus make the journey with her, she will not be able to say "Ah, I'd rather stay," so as not to embarrass you ...

It is a high level of manipulation to spend a little time with, not a technique that I recommend, of course. Real seducers don't need tricks like that to attract women.

The A, B or C meeting

My favorite. The brain is fascinating! A girl you have planned to see again, suggests an appointment A or B, A being an option that suits her, B being her favorite.

If she wants to give him the feeling of freedom and give him the illusion of a decision, she can introduce a completely excruciating choice C.

"Dear, tonight I offer Batman vs. Superman, or Civil War, or Visitors 3: YOU choose!"

Handling level "nice," to see the movies she wants, and go to restaurants that make her happy. It also works for the great "sea or mountain" debate for the summer holidays!

Only qualities

This manipulation technique is questionable; we talk about the white lie, lying by omission. I recently read an article in the NY TIMES: should you reveal your mental illnesses on a first date?

Children? It's not a fault, and you can talk about it!

A cleaner criminal record? She neither! (And then you paid your debt to the company, normally.)

An old pervasive love? You don't have to tell her your ex is harassing you.

If you hide something that bothers you a little, there will always be time to tell her later. If she discovers it—you were too in love with her and that you did not want to lose her.

Handling rate: 50-50, it all depends on the defect you are trying to hide. Forgivable? 50-50, it all depends on the emotional shock it will cause him/her!

Body language synchronization

The easiest, most visual technique you can find in the trailer for the film "LE COACH" with Jean-Paul Rouve and Richard Berry.

Wait for fatigue to persuade better

This, with age, seems to be more and more harmful.

Have you ever tried playing tired poker? Your ability to make decisions is ridiculous. This is why poker players must sleep during major tournaments and do not mess around in the nightclub during games.

When you hit the nightclub, it's a bit like after four in the morning. Alcohol and fatigue impair your judgment, like that of the girl you like (you like four grams, we all agree).

Trying to seduce a tired girl is a manipulation. We are not aware of it when we are young since everyone is exploded by alcohol and fatigue, but it is a mode of operation accepted by student life.

The fear strategy

Techniques-manipulation-seduction-fear

The media feed on fear. The news, on TV: more than 80% of deaths, attacks, strikes, unemployment, all bad news.

On the manipulation side, some men are very strong at explaining to their prey that they will end up on their own, that they are worthless, and that they do not deserve to be looked at.

These types are generally "narcissistic perverts," as they are mentioned in magazines. They know how to find the woman's weak point in front of them and press it.

It is a strategy generally used to recover them when a woman threatens to leave or has left them. And often effective, unfortunately. These guys are slowly destroying the self-confidence that the woman had in her ... until she only relies on the man.

Be honest, as much as possible. Be direct, be frank. You don't have to lie to women to seduce or sleep with them. On the other hand, you must become more interesting and more exciting!

CROWD MANIPULATION

Manipulation techniques to influence people and get everything you want.

Manipulating someone to get something you want can easily be categorized as evil or even cowardly.

That's why you have to be honest with me and promise something to me: you wouldn't use such methods for evil purposes.

Place your right hand on your side, and with me repeat:

"I do not use such methods of deception for negative reasons."

Those methods have been medically accepted, often based on more than 20 years of study! But I won't go in-depth here, because I don't want to make your life more difficult.

I'm showing you the strategy, quick to clarify it, and we're moving on to the next. Simple as a trot. No more complications. No fuss at all.

You may want to negotiate your salary... maybe you want to influence your friends to make a short weekend trip ... or maybe you want to negotiate a discount for a purchase you want to make.

No matter what your motivation, the seven manipulation techniques we are about to share with you WORK and have proven themselves.

1: Get Someone to Help You

This technique is also called the Benjamin Franklin Effect, and it's so simple that it works every time.

Benjamin Franklin genuinely tried to "settle the scores" with a guy who despised him for the record.

BF asked this guy to lend him a rare book and graciously thanked him when he got it. The product of the races was his best mate, this guy who did not even want to talk to BF.

Scientists wanted to test this hypothesis and discovered that researchers who asked for a personal favor were given a higher ranking than researchers who did not ask for a personal favor.

In short: if anyone gives you a favor, it's because they're sure you're a good guy.

In a seduction context, if you want to seduce someone, ask them to do a little service for you.

Simple as Hello.

2: Foot in the door

The Foot in the Door technique stipulates making a ridiculous request, which will push the person you want to manipulate to refuse, then, right after, you make a less ridiculous or rather logical request, and your target will end up accepting because that person feels a little bad about refusing your first request.

Example: You ask your mate to lend you a weekend with his Ferrari. He refuses. A few hours later you come back and ask him to lend you 100€. Bingo. And bingo. No complications, he sends you the 100€.

Another one. A child begs his father to give him €50 pocket money a week instead of €10, and the father declines. The same evening, the child asks his father to go and spend the night with his friend—the father agrees.

3: Use the person's first name often

The next time when you meet your buddy, instead of saying, "Hi man," say: "Hi David, it's been a while," and throughout your conversation, put his first name here and there—and you'll notice he's more attentive.

If you are in a store, perhaps negotiating a carpet, ask for the seller's first name, and say:

"Look, Samir. I know I'm a tourist, but that doesn't mean you can sell me this rug at this high price. You seem to be an honest person, Samir. Let's close this matter without making life difficult. I give you the price of [...]"

Friendly tip: Reduce this price by 50%. Otherwise, go to the next store ;)

4: Flattery

Well executed, flattery can work miracles.

If you know how to flatter someone, you can manipulate them as you see fit, provided your flattery is sincere. It's very important.

If you throw compliments just to flatter that person, then the opposite effect can easily happen. Instead of making someone appreciate you, they will hate you.

5: The "Mirroring"

The Mirroring, known as the effect of the mirror, simply states to adopt the same body language of the person you want to manipulate/influence.

Repeat the same gestures, the same sentences/words, and if you want to go even further—repeat the same rhythm of breathing. It's crazy, I know. But the pros do this all the time.

Let's say you are meeting with your boss, and you are negotiating your salary increase ... once in his office, notice how he is sitting, and do the same. If he crosses his arms or feet, do the same, etc.

6: Door to nose

It is the opposite technique to the foot in the door technique. This time, instead of making a ridiculous request, you are going to make a request that he cannot refuse. In the film "The Godfather," they talk about "An Offer they can't refuse."

7: Silence is golden

Here is the method: Instead of getting into a heated debate, listen to what this person has to say to you and then try to understand how they feel and, especially why...

Trigger social pressure

How to overcome social pressure?

Where does this social pressure come from? Why does it exist and persist from generation to generation?

To understand where social pressure comes from, you must understand by whom it is exercised, to understand the motivations behind it. It comes from 6 sources:

- Our parents
- Other family members
- The media
- Teachers, guidance counselors, schools
- Businesses

Each of these sources has its reasons for maintaining social pressure:

1: Our parents

Our parents want the best for us and want us to be safe. Their intentions are a priori good when they push us to choose elite professional paths. It is because they tell themselves that by doing this, we will have the security of a permanent contract, that we will be able to climb the ladder and have financial security. With all that, we should live well and not end up on the street.

I'll give you an example. My friend's father was born during the Second World War. When he was little, he was hungry because he did not have much money to buy food. Later in his professional life, he experienced different situations. He was employed but also craftsman on his account. He experienced the difficulties of being self-employed, so when he returned to CDI in business, it brought him some security. Because of this story, I understand that her father encouraged his to find a permanent contract, to have a job well placed, to be able to have some security, and potentially a better retirement than him.

If your parents are one of the people who put pressure on you or let's say, make you go this way, try to learn more about their story: why are they so attached to your success?

2: Other family members

Parents are a special case because they have the mission to raise and help us survive in this world. But sometimes other family members also tell us about our orientation and try to give us advice. What is their motivation? It depends on who it is. Some live by proxy: they would like to see us accomplish something that they could not accomplish, to see us go further than them so that they can be proud of that. This applies to grandparents, cousins, uncles and aunts, older brothers and sisters, who have chosen a different path and are curious to see someone in the family, succeed in this path.

3: The media

To get an audience, the media need to choose topics that will provoke emotions and reactions. For them, it will work more to say "Who are these students of the elite: one day in the life of a student of HEC." By introducing mystery, they give a kind of mysticism around the phenomenon of "elite classes." If they said, "We are going to meet the students of a business school," we would say "Yeah, so what?" But to place HEC students as special people, who have accomplished something special, it's much more sensational, and we want to know the history.

4: The state

The state has an interest in training geniuses, to be able to compete with other countries in technical fields, and companies earn more money and increase the country's GDP, which strengthens the country's image of power. The state has an interest in promoting the elite to make them want to continue and go further. All this can be felt or heard in speeches. Well, after that, it probably depends on the President's political party.

5: Education and guidance professionals

When a teacher sees a good student, he wants to help him go as far as possible. Because it is part of his mission, and it can bring him a little personal pride to have helped to raise this person.

The guidance counselors are a reflection of the overall functioning: if they see a good student, they send him to the elite classes because that's what they do.

Then there are also schools. They are interested in helping us succeed in increasing their popularity and continue to have students who register each year to continue to exist. This is all the more typical in private establishments, such as the Business Schools, which have partnerships with large companies, which come to seek their future employees in schools. In itself, everyone is there: students have easier internships and jobs because they benefit from the reputation of the school and the partnership, companies have quality candidates, and students and businesses fund the school. But it is a little biased because the school encourages to join certain types of companies, and favors less other ways, such as entrepreneurship.

6: Businesses

It ties in with the sixth source of pressure: businesses. When they recruit, having a certain diploma is a recruitment criterion. And sometimes even having only the diploma of the first three grades Écoles. To have a job in a good company, a renowned company, you must, therefore, have the diploma that allows you to access it.

7: Ourselves

Finally, the last source of pressure, which I kept secret, is... ourselves. And there you have to be surprised and tell yourself, "How am I a source of the pressure that I feel from the outside?" Well, because of all the other sources of previous pressure, I believe that we internalize the concept of the social scale, the idea that one must obtain a diploma, such a diploma, the best diploma.

If this concept seemed to us to be unacceptable, we would violently reject it. But we don't reject it, because somewhere we believe in it. And we believe in it because we evolve with everything we are told: our parents, our uncle or our grandmother, our teachers, the media, etc. So, by being told about certain success ideas, we learn to believe it ourselves, and we live with it.

Exercise: Before moving on, I suggest you ask yourself the following questions: Who do you feel social pressure from? In what form? What do these people say or have told you? How do you feel when they tell you that? Why do you think you feel that?

How to overcome social pressure?

We would like to help you get over that. Operate according to your real needs, not according to the gaze of others and social pressure because it is one of the main brakes that prevent us from being fulfilled at work.

Why can't we detach ourselves from social pressure: 4 reasons?

The question we can ask ourselves is: why is it so difficult for us to detach ourselves from this social pressure, to make decisions without taking them into account?

When we feel that the functioning no longer suits us, that we are aware that this concept of social hierarchy influences us and that there are trades that are better than others, why can't we make decisions other than under the influence of this concept?

The seductive art

Meeting someone and generally trying to have a specific effect on that person creates anxiety for most people, those just beginning to date and even those "experienced" in the dating field. There is something that triggers your body's hormones into sudden overdrive, but what you do after this trigger counts. Some people tend to be unsure about what to do next, even after having made the initial contact with the opposite sex. But others don't waste time in the art of seduction once the connection has been made.

In different cultures and different groups of people, seduction stands for different things. While seduction produces visions of passion and emotional intimacy for some people and induces a sense of excitement, sensuality, and sexual desire, most people don't like the thought of "seducing." For many others, the concept of seduction creates fear of being tricked, abused, and sexually harassed. It usually implies that the seducer behaves out of a motive other than a desire for the seducer and that such actions would not necessarily be the focus of seduction.

In recent decades, attempts to make our culture more sex-positive have only created viciously cynical rhetoric that has resulted in further intensifying our distrust of the art of seduction as something dangerous, damaging and detrimental to us as individuals and to society as a whole.

Seduction in modern society combines with deceit, trickery, selfishness, manipulation, pretense, and a play on words. One gets seduced by a lover, a salesman, a politician, or an artist's promises. Seduction seems to be designed to trick one into reality, talking nonsense. We see this sort of seduction celebrated as entertainment and advertised as a commodity full of pornographic images, narrative, and symbolism. We see it in the newspapers, film, music videos, office, education. At philosophical seminars, it is even learned that it is nearly impossible to escape it in everyday life—most actors and stars owe their fame to their seduction mastery.

This disenchanted interpretation of seduction as a desire to act out the body as something that can't wait to be undressed, has even infiltrated our sexual relations. Seduction has, in most cases, nothing to do with love or even being attracted to the other person. Rather, it is about getting something through the use of deception and trickery—such as sex or financial favors. Many of us are suffering from their catastrophic influence. It would be easy to point out many areas where our attempts at the art of seduction are more manipulative and selfish than loving and selfless.

From a very young age, most people learn the power of exploitative seduction by using seduction to get what they want from their parents and siblings, special favors from the teacher and other children. It begins when a child is often shy, nervous, and doesn't feel confident about him or herself, conscious that by seducing others, they can get attention from those they seduce. In some cases, this recognition gives the child a sense of self-worth. The child feels like the other person likes him or her by seduction because they pay more attention, offer, and do things that make the child feel different. But that is a false self-worth feeling. If they can't seduce someone, they feel unworthy, and so they step up their seduction.

They continue this pattern as they grow older and switch on this seduction automatically when they want something from someone. They feel good when they can seduce others, but at the heart of their being, self-worth depends on whether or not they can seduce another. Seduction feeds on their lack of self-worth, lack of self-confidence, lack of self-esteem. If they can't seduce them, they feel indignant. Some people have made this art great, which they are not yet consciously aware of.

When we seduce in this way, it's just a false sense of power based on someone else that allows us to seduce them. When we're seduced by exploitation, we gave the seducer our power. It takes away from naturalness, "fact," and the whole essence of the seduction art's inspiring qualities. A person in his or her power, full of self-love and self-worth, need not be seduced in a manipulative manner, nor can they be seduced by manipulation.

Are frustrating, superficial, mechanical, predictable, manipulative, selfish, emotionally disconnected relationships void of passion, and increased intimacy inevitable given the fact that manipulative seduction has impregnated our modern world? Can we lift our hands and never expect to have the unique transformative well of strength, regeneration, and spiritual elevation provided by the art of seduction?

No! Former seduction art practitioners were so amazed at the power of this energy that they were convinced that it was the secret of youth, health, and vitality.

Our human nature isn't so skewed we can't do our part. The evolutionary work had, in fact, already started. Modern versions of "old rituals and practices" give a glimpse of what the seduction art once was to modern audiences. Nonetheless, as we start to believe that this is the only way to connect with the opposite sex, we fall into the trap of memorized pick-up lines and automatic seduction scripts that take from us the very power that makes the art of seduction so inherently effective. We invariably lose both the heart and soul of the seduction phenomenon and, thus, our connection to one of the deepest and deeper aspects of human fulfillment.

It is time to demystify and rehabilitate the ancient art of seduction and take advantage of its mega-power. The whole mystery of this timeless ritual, forgotten and long misunderstood, may well be what we need today to rescue us from the current erotic famine, get our groove back on, and the fire back in our groins.

Subliminal Techniques, seduction

I'm going to start here in an unusual way by telling you about the subliminal messages you're not going to hear from ANY other. In reality, you are NOT the body. You are a spirit riding in your body, and you co-use the organic brain of your body, but your essential intellect comes from the etheric realm of eternity. The native brain of your body is wrongly labeled as your subconscious mind. If indeed, the subconscious mind is the thinking of the organic human, a human without a soul is a moderately intelligent animal, but an ape is no longer capable of more complex thought.

This controversial presumption stems from the death experience, where most of the intellect traveled on to eternity after drowning the human component. It only stands to reason that if the bulk of the mind transcends mortality, then real intelligence can't be a complete function of the human body.

You may wonder, 'what in the hell does this have to do with subliminal techniques of seduction?' The reaction is clear. Either male or female, the human-animal wants to match, and it has no morals against even coupling in a street corner like a dog. The morality against this type of behavior is a spirit feature that functions as the conscious mind. When you use subliminal tactics, you try to communicate to the human-animal directly and bypass the conscious spirit ego. Acceptance of this as true will greatly improve your subliminal manipulation efficacy.

You might have a firm grasp of the complexities of language, but the communication skills of the organic person are dramatically reduced. This is why the subconscious mind continues to misinterpret synonyms and phrases that are more nuanced.

I try to use the term 'behind me' when I talk to a lady whom I want to seduce. It's something that can be introduced into almost any conversation unnoticeably. IE: 'The use of that seduction tactic is below me.' The conscious mind of the girl will interpret the meaning exactly as I said it, but the marginal human thinking capacity below will get it as the subliminal message of 'blow me' as in an oral sex request, because it sounds about the same when the 'be' is not stressed enough. You may have noticed that almost all vulgar sex terms (usually only 4-letters) are short. Is it so that human beings can learn and obey?

Just one insertion of 'blow me' is unlikely to translate into a full-blown seduction immediately, but when it is one of the numerous sexual innuendos subliminally fired off, the human female's irresistible mating urge will eventually override restraints artificially placed by the soul intellect of the girl. Then the subliminal tactics' seduction will prove to be completely successful.

CHAPTER 12
MANAGEMENT OF DIVERSITY

Diversity is now a priority for several organizations. Beneficial from the ethical and economic angles, it remains a daily challenge on the ground. Managers must agree to review their practices while developing new management skills. Let's see how to support them through this organizational change.

In 2006, the French firm Sodexo made diversity a strategic axis and an organizational priority. "She has invested thousands of hours of training, she has created programs dedicated to inclusion and, above all, she has given herself quantified objectives," explains Vincent Calvez, professor of management at the Graduate School of Business Sciences. Two years later, an independent survey showed that only 40% of employees perceived this approach positively.

Since then, Sodexo has been able to rally its employees to the cause, and the company has won several diversity awards. But his example shows two things. First, engaging an organization in an inclusion project is a long-term job. Second, middle managers, who are in daily contact with employees, have a crucial role in integrating and building diversity into the organization, so every effort should be made to develop their skills in this regard.

Develop "intercultural" skills

In her training on cultural diversity, Brigitte Lavallée, CRHA, diversity and inclusion consultant, seeks to develop empathy by guiding the participants in an exercise in which they must imagine having to leave Quebec, move with their whole family, leave to zero and overcome many obstacles.

"Empathy is an extremely important quality to develop in a context of diversity management," she explains. To get there, you have to be able to walk in each other's shoes.

Another way to develop empathy for marginalized employees is to gain basic knowledge of their reality. "Research shows us that we approach work in different ways according to countries and cultures," says Johanne St-Onge, CHRP, founding president of the RHRE consulting firm. For example, the relationship to time and hierarchy may differ from country to country and from culture to culture. Hence, the training's usefulness was to introduce managers to the differences in culture and gender or the reality of people with disabilities.

Managers also need to get to know themselves. "This is one aspect of individual coaching," explains Johanne St-Onge. A manager must be fully aware of his expectations if he is to explain them to his employees successfully.

Next, managers who wish to develop their diversity management skills should consider a communication component. "Communication is an essential element in managing diversity," recalls Vincent Calvez. Exchange and dialogue make it possible to establish a bond of trust between the hierarchy and its staff. They also help defuse emerging tensions and minimize conflicts.

To develop skills in diversity management, it is better to diversify educational resources and tools. "We know that individuals do not all learn the same way," notes Brigitte Lavallée. "Some have an analytical mind. Others learn best by observation, case studies, or trial and error."

How to overcome resistance

When a company engages in the process of diversity and inclusion, many concerns rise to the surface. Brigitte Lavallée sees it on the ground. "Some managers tell me: in Rome, we do like the Romans. This suggests that immigrants should integrate by adopting ways of doing things in the organization.

However, practicing inclusion requires being willing to question yourself, to listen, and to enrich yourself through the diversity of points of view."

In light of her research, Tania Saba, CHRP, full professor of the BMO Chair in Diversity and Governance at the University of Montreal, notes that there is still a long way to go. "When we look at the demographic representation of management teams, we are far from seeing a proportional representation of immigrants, women, people with disabilities, and Aboriginals," she says.

The professor notes that the organizations that are most successful in their inclusion process are those whose management demonstrates unequivocal leadership.

She cited the example of the outgoing President of VIA Rail, Yves Desjardins-Siciliano when he wanted to achieve parity in his management team, which included only 11% of women. "Since I did not have time to convince everyone," he said at a conference in which Tania Saba participated, I decreed that from now on, for all management positions, we should have a man and woman as final candidates. And if the woman was not chosen, I should be told why the man was the best candidate.

Learn to correct bias

In a context of diversity, explains Brigitte Lavallée, human beings sometimes draw conclusions based on their biases and prejudices. For example, we tend to interpret conflicting situations between individuals by their culture, age, or gender difference when it is perhaps simply a difference in personality regardless of an identity group.

"I suggest bringing managers to treat each employee as a unique person, rather than seeing them through the characteristics of their identity group," explains the consultant.

She also made a point: "Managers often take care to treat everyone equally so as not to create injustice. However, in a context of diversity, what prevails is equity, which is to offer everyone the same chances of access to a favorable work environment, promotions, and training."

A participative management model to promote inclusion?

Managers cannot simply develop their "interpersonal" skills to manage diversity on an individual basis better. They must also demonstrate leadership on the organizational level by learning innovative management practices likely to better respond to the reality of a plural work team.

One of these practices aims at a management mode centered on employee participation in the decision-making process. "In an inclusive philosophy, a company must be ready to listen to what its employees have to say," explains Brigitte Lavallée. It suggests setting up advisory committees where employees can express their concerns while helping to find solutions.

Vincent Calvez adds, citing a case he uses in progress: "For diversity to function, collaborate and move forward without crisis, a French firm has opted for what is called smart working. This is to leave freedom of organization and schedules to employees, while empowering them on the objectives to be achieved and the work to be done, and bringing them together through a commonplace of work. This collaborative model is not always possible, but it suggests a way forward." Johanne St-Onge proposes the image of a tree: "It is important to have a common trunk, but you also have to know how to let the branches of the tree extend. People must be able to express their diversity. This is the challenge of a society that has chosen a model of intercultural integration.

CHAPTER 13
CONCEPT OF DECEPTION

Deceit is an act of assertion that misleads, conceals the facts, or encourages a false perception, principle, or idea. Sometimes, this is achieved for personal advantage or benefit. Deception can involve concealment, propaganda, and sleight of hand, as well as distraction, camouflage, or disguise. There is also self-disappointment, as in bad faith. It may also be named, with various contextual implications: beguilement, deception, hoax, mystification, ruse, or subterfuge.

Deception is a major transgression in relationships and often leads to feelings of alienation and mistrust between the relationship partners. Deception violates the rules of relationships and is seen as a negative breach of expectations. Most people tend to be honest much of the time with relatives, intimate partners, and even strangers. If people expected most interactions to be untruthful, it would take confusion and misdirection to obtain reliable information while chatting and engaging with others. Between some romantic and relational partners, a considerable amount of deception occurs.

Deceit and dishonesty can also constitute grounds for civil litigation in tort or contract law (where, if deliberately, it is known as misrepresentation or fraudulent misrepresentation) or cause criminal prosecution for fraud. It also forms a vital part of Denial and Deception in psychological warfare.

TYPES OF DECEPTION

Deception encompasses several types of communications or omissions that distort or omit the entire truth. Examples of deception include misrepresentations and misleading claims that omit relevant information, leading the receiver to infer false conclusions. For example, a claim that 'sunflower oil is beneficial for brain health because of the presence of omega-3 fatty acids' can be misleading. It leads the recipient to believe that sunflower oil will benefit brain health more than other foods. Sunflower oil's omega-3 fatty acids are relatively small and are not especially good for brain wellbeing. Although this claim is technically true, it induces the recipient to infer false information. Deception itself manages verbal or nonverbal messages intentionally so that the receiver of the message will believe in a way that the sender knows is false. The intent of the deception is critical. Purpose distinguishes between deceit and an honest mistake. The Interpersonal Deception Theory explores the interrelation of cognitions and behaviors in deceptive exchanges between the communicative context and the sender and receiver.

Some forms of deception include:

Lies: To make up facts or to provide facts which are contrary or somewhat different from the reality.

Equivocations: Making a statement of indirectness, ambiguity, or contradiction.

Concealments: Omitting significant or appropriate information for the given purpose, or engaging in conduct that seeks to conceal relevant information.

Exaggerations: A distortion or, to any extent twisting the facts.

Understatements: They minimize or downplay aspects of the truth.

Untruthful: Often referred to as misinterpreting the truth.

Many people think they're good at deception, though this trust is often misplaced.

MOTIVES FOR DECEPTION

- Instrumental: escaping retribution or conserving capital.
- Relational: maintaining ties or links.
- Identity: retain "name" or an image of oneself.

Best Deception methods

"It consists of telling lies and some hidden truths in the form of a joke. After an embarrassing act, we end up saying: "Deception! " A term that we use when we can no longer explain or argue. This term can also be juxtaposed with other words and even phrases or expressions we can say, for example: "Deceit was I going to do such a thing ..." or "deception (+ infinitive)."

Deception reduced in itself is absurd; it is only the expression of a personal will to apologize to others. With deception, we seek an excuse for everything we do awkwardly.

Deception is contagious between people who sometimes suffer from insecurity. If it is not insecurity, it is, therefore, a pure deception, since the deceptions fall certain times at the right time. It is here that it is no longer insecurity but a temporal reality.

It is also a way of putting our faults and our problems into perspective. Deception thus makes us assume in a funny, even puerile way, reality. Thus, the technique of deception becomes interesting, since it has this capacity to allow the individual to take his problems more gently with this playful spirit, to get out of it and overcome the boredom which troubles him, and prevents him from falling into discomfort.

The word deception has its origins in play and the minds of adolescents. Through deception, teens translate their indefinable character since they are in a transition phase in which they seek their own identity and feel incomprehension. However, we must beware, because deception can lead us to mediocrity and a lifestyle based on lies for the sole pleasure of lying.

In very particular cases, the practice of this technique can be negative, for example, when it deprives the individual of the knowledge of a truth which he needs since it was created to betray the consciences of others.

Deception is also "socializing" when it is pointed out to others. In this case, deception becomes a more enjoyable and fun way to report the error to the other person, because the other feels somehow understood and accepted (in the majority of cases). This understanding will be able to be the basis of a good friendship.

CHAPTER 14
THE ART OF PERSUASION

Persuasion is a difficult art, and I know something about it because most of my attempts to change the position of others fail: long speeches full of passion seem to reach their goal, but fail to persuade. What a joy, for me, to discover one day the existence of a particular type of influence, which psychologists call persuasion.

Some are more gifted at persuasion than others. As with any other human faculty, there is a continuum of talent. At one end are those who always fail in their attempts to persuade; on the other, there are the "super-shaders," who always succeed. Who are these gifted? It is difficult to characterize them, but when you meet one, there is no way to go wrong.

Simplicity above all

The situation was tense, but a few simple words were enough to avoid the conflict. Without knowing it, the character who relaxed the atmosphere had associated psychology, biology, and neuroscience within a model comprising five factors united in the acronym spice: simplicity and perception of one's interest.

PRINCIPLES OF PERSUASION TO CONVINCE ANYONE

1: Manipulation

When we try to get something from a person, we unknowingly use principles of persuasion, including manipulation. Manipulation, which is often wrongly a global term, and which is not a principle of persuasion but the set of all the mechanisms, is, a strong principle. Manipulation involves obtaining what one wants from a person without them realizing that one has used weapons of influence. Like all principles of influences, manipulation should be used ethically and for ethical purposes.

2: Pooling

Pooling involves creating debt between another person and us. This technique of influence is based on the principle of reciprocity, which means that when we receive something from someone, we feel obliged to return the favor back to them. With this technique, we will, therefore, make the person feel indebted to us. Of course, it is about offering something symbolic, something that has value, but not too much either. The goal is that the person can give us something superior.

3: Involvement

Have you ever noticed that when you commit to doing something, it's very difficult to reverse your decision? This principle is called Commitment and Coherence, and I chose the term of implication because this term alone evokes this principle. When we get involved in something, we will try to go all the way, first for us, for all the efforts we have made and not to pass for a weather vane opposite to our loved ones, friends, or family.

4: The recommendation

What do you do when you want to dine at a restaurant you've never been to? You send a message to a friend who may have already eaten there, or you will see the reviews on the Internet, or maybe both. That's how humans need to have the advice of others to do or think something. You can think for yourself, but to make a decision, we all like to have the recommendation of other people. It is also what made social networks popular.

5: Affection

We need to appreciate to buy, well most of the time at least. A waiter at the restaurant who has been friendly throughout the meal will often have more tips than a rude waiter. It is on this principle that the waiters in American restaurants think of all the best. They are only paid for tips most of the time and are therefore obliged to be both professional and friendly to have the best tips possible.

6: Specialization

A human cannot be good in all areas. This is how specializations are created, to be able to train experts in certain specialties. If the company were not configured like this, we would be able to do a lot of things, but we would not be experts in our trades since we would not deepen the various subjects. There would, therefore, be no surgeons, sanitary installers, or pastry chefs. In this specialization society, we are therefore obliged to trust people who are recognized as experts in their field.

7: Valuation

Valuation is the act of adding value to a product or service by presenting it in a certain way. That is to say that two identical products presented differently will be seen differently by potential buyers. This is the principle of scarcity, but I wanted to evoke further the principle of valuation, which encompasses several techniques of persuasion, including scarcity. Improving the offer is important, but improving the presentation of the offer is even more important!

8: Automation

In a society that is going faster and faster, and where decisions must often be taken immediately, instant influence is more than ever used by our brain. It is essential to understand this principle of influence both to convince and not to be fooled by scammers, but also by the media who abuse this mechanism of influence, perhaps even without their knowledge. Automation is about giving an immediate answer to a question, behavior, or anything else.

Examples of Persuasion in Real Life, in Your Relationship, Work, and Love

The key steps and the original exercise to convince a man!

If there is indeed a problem for women when they are married, it is that they often find it difficult to impose their choices or their ideas in front of their partner.

Do you want to take a step further, have a child, get married, settle in with him, but he doesn't think the same way you do? Your companion insists on refusing, and it is often he who has the last word, both for the less important projects and those that are particularly close to your heart. Do not give way to despair and acceptance of this situation. There is no point in letting time run out because nothing will work out that way. You have to take the lead and not lose time because you can persuade a man by learning the right techniques.

The importance of making your ideas heard

I can never say it enough; self-confidence is the key to happiness in any area, be it family life, professional life, or as in this case, in matters of sentimental life. There is no limit to this area of concern to us, far from it. Indeed, insurance is needed in your married life. Not only to fully live through your romantic relationship but also to, sometimes, know how to stand up to your man when you cannot get your ideas across, or when your latter acts in a way that you dislike. Unfortunately, many women cannot convince a man because they dare not defend their opinions and are pessimistic about changing their minds.

Make your ideas heard, don't be afraid to express yourself, and suggesting changes for your relationship should not be a fear. If you are doing this, it is because you feel that your relationship needs it. However, you must realize that the relationships between men/women in love are different. If your man never shares your opinion, it is not necessarily a "punishment" against you, and it is that he has another vision of life and happiness.

The Don'ts to Convince a Man

Do you think this strategy is very effective in settling critical conflicts?

Imagine you want to move in with your boyfriend for a moment to have a "normal" life as a couple, but the latter refuses. Will depriving him of sex sincerely make him change his mind and convince him to want to live with his girlfriend?

The second scenario proves that this technique quickly knows its limits. If you want to be a mother, are you going to deprive your companion of sex? The answer is obvious. It is, therefore, absolutely not the method to use!

To convince a man, you have to ask the right questions. So you have to ask yourself: Will you have to ask him or push him to change? Because in reality, nothing prevents him from telling you he agrees, sleeping with you, and changing your mind immediately after the act. I might seem a little caricatured, but it's already happened. I think sincerity is the foundation of a happy couple and that coercing a man is not necessarily the right method.

If you want changes, it's for your couple's benefit or your partner won't be happy if you pushed him to make a decision. As you have just learned, an ultimatum can be incredibly dangerous for your love life under these circumstances.

How to persuade a man to change in love

For things to evolve, it is, therefore, through concrete and thoughtful actions that you can convince a man and make him change his mind. Communication is the main weapon for sharing ideas in a relationship. You need to have a frank discussion with your man to make him understand that he cannot decide alone. Be careful; however, threats do not work in these situations, so there is no need to say "be careful, if you do not change, I will leave you" because that would have no impact.

Just prove to him that it is a real need for you and that you must take this step together to give additional importance to your relationship. Contrary to popular belief and caricatures that can be seen in some media, men are not content only with video games, football, and beer. They also need to have a stable and fulfilling life as a couple to be completely happy.

The technique that will change your man

Now I am going to offer you an exercise that offers spectacular results to convince a man.

Take a blank sheet for this, and first, you must list what you would like to improve yourself.

Then, on another sheet, write the reasons why you would like these changes to take place.

Finally, you will have to take another sheet, and you will have to list all the advantages that this change can bring to your relationship.

This will allow you to have a basis for reflection and prepare for the discussion you want to have with your other half. To convince a man, it is not necessary to shout or make threats. Just present your arguments to him, and you will see that his position will evolve naturally.

To prepare for possible remarks, anticipate your man's questions by remembering to list the negative points to immediately answer them and do not let him impose himself again.

CHAPTER 15
PERSUASION LESSONS FROM A FOUR-YEAR-OLD CHILD

The 4-year-old is more independent. He feels capable and can control his strength and security. He likes to feel part of the housework and takes care of his things. He manages to wash his hands and face, put away his clothes, fix the sheets on his bed, brush his teeth, and pick up his toys in the room and all... he alone! She has a great relationship with her friends and loves to invite them to her house.

He can go up and down the stairs more easily, participate in competitive games, and be ready to play anything. Show preferences for clothes, hairstyles, food, and friends.

- He begins to ask questions about all the aspects that make him curious and will show some interest in his birth and death. He loves looking at photographs and watching movies from when he was little.

- In his level of thought, an evolution is perceived, since he can classify objects and materials by color, shape, or number. But not only that, he is already located in space and includes the notions "outside," "inside," "above," "below". Likewise, he also narrates experiences of daily life and does so with greater fluency and better pronunciation.

At four years old, challenges begin for children

At this age, the child presents instability in his emotions. He laughs and cries for no apparent reason, and that causes him to return, from time to time, to the tantrums of two years of age. He wants to impose his wishes by challenging his parents. The four-year-old boy will feel a special preference for his mother if he is a boy, identifying with the father and competing with him for his mother. However, the girl will show weakness for her father and will act in the same way as the boy.

It is a stage in which parents must have a lot of patience, tact, and control of the situation. Let us not forget that we are dealing with a young child, who has a very limited capacity for understanding, and it is we, the parents, who must teach him little by little. Other than that, he will start with the why's. He will look for answers, and it is convenient always to answer him truthfully. By responding to a child, we are teaching him to think, and we are helping to form the basis of his worldview.

Mastering Subconscious Persuasiveness to Attain Everything You Want

Subconscious persuasion is a matter of great

significance, as it will get you out of many difficult circumstances if you master it. Okay, different people use various manipulation techniques to get others to do the things that they want to do, using physical force, a cajoling tone and even using strong language. You could use persuasion as an instrument at home, at work, and so on to accomplish your various goals in life and, more so, to achieve the joy you've always been looking for.

Learning the influence of subconscious persuasion will place you in a position to gain insight when using the tricks of persuasion. What you need to learn about the power of persuasion is that it primarily uses the internalized ability of persuasion and reading the thoughts and actions of others. Such factors make the whole process a breeze, with fantastic outcomes promised.

Master subconscious persuasion to do whatever you want to achieve

You currently have other methods that you can use to start the subconscious persuasion process into the mechanics. Second, you have to look at your accent. It has been shown that when you want to communicate to your subconscious mind, the use of a voice which is a little lower when talking to someone is more successful. The use of a low voice has the effect of calming the person and lowering their defenses, more importantly. This eventually leads to the establishment of a trust in these individuals.

Subliminal technology, as a therapy

Subliminal technology is one of the most successful treatments which can be used to enhance persuasion power. That's because this one is directed at the brain, and better yet, it's also important to note that any activity that happens within and in the body is regulated in the brain. Researching for more information is, therefore, key. There are a lot of resources for subliminal technology. They're going to teach you how it can be used to improve subliminal persuasion. You learn as much as you can.

Below are basic techniques for overcoming subconscious persuasion.

Framing technique: No better way to adjust the system of categorizing, arranging, associating, and ultimately giving meaning to all aspects of life, from objects to things, or even actions, than this one. Framing has the purpose of moving viewers to the viewpoints and using terms that conjure up images in the minds of those you're presenting to construct persuasive arguments.

The mirroring technique is a representation of the actions (body language and movements) of the group you use in persuasion. What you do is create a sense of compassion by playing the role of the audience. This technique, also known as the Chameleon Effect, is more powerful because you use it subconsciously.

Timing technique: Researchers have shown Implicit Manipulation to be particularly effective when practiced by individuals with a rather brain cracking operation. If you speak to a person about things that they do not consent to, remember beginning the conversation when that particular person is emotionally drained.

The strategy of reciprocation: We are greatly constrained by the good deeds of the near people in our lives. Possibly, if you're doing something sweet to your friend, at home, or work, they're always going to do you well for reciprocation. What you will achieve by this is that you will balance these partnerships with the influence of the Subconscious Persuasion.

Restricted Uses of Reciprocity as an Effective Persuasive Technique

How do you want an easy and rapid Persuasive Technique to make others believe that they are "important" to you? Imagine a strategy of persuasion that would mean for a sales call, a sales letter (yes, you can even do it in writing), a meeting, a business conversation, or a situation where you are trying to convince someone to do something.

There's a simple way you can create a sense of duty in someone. You do this by applying the principle of reciprocity. When you give something to someone, the person will almost always feel obliged to give you something back. The sense of reciprocity is so high that in research studies where one person treated people kindly and the other person treated the same people poorly but gave them something (let's say they offered soda), they were more likely to do something for the person who treated them poorly. Reciprocity is one of the most powerful techniques of convincing you can use.

So, if you're familiar with interchange, don't stop reading, because, in a few minutes, I've got a little different twist on this whole idea to share with you.

It's very likely that when you think about reciprocity, you think of giving a "thing" to someone ... It could be a gift, a meal, a drink, or some other physical object. The problem with this is that in business situations, existing ethical guidelines can preclude gifts (this is certainly the case in government contracts). In personal and business contexts, providing a physical object creates a sense of duty to provide something in exchange that can sometimes be uncomfortable.

Have you ever received a gift from someone at Christmas but don't have anything to give in return? Next thing you know, you're sneaking out of the house to run down to the store or looking in the closet for the gifts left over. Reciprocity is not necessarily an efficient method of reasoning because it is applied in the wrong manner at the wrong time.

Another way to build an urge to reciprocate is to invest some of the time on someone else.

The problem with doing something for others is that this method of persuasion won't work in cases where you don't have the chance to use it because of time constraints or other reasons, or you may not want to make an effort.

Another way of inducing the persuasion technique of reciprocity is to exchange information. The most common approach to do this is to exchange information the other party does not have (and would consider valuable). As a marketer, when I made sales calls to prospective customers, I would almost always seek and have some knowledge that the consumer would consider useful. I would often give starters some early guidance on how to change new ads and make it work better. Another strategy I found useful would be to say to the prospect something they didn't know about their rivals or their customers' buying preferences.

A comment on ethics is important here, by the way. Do not share information that is not suitable for giving away. This is information given to you in confidentiality, sensitive or proprietary information to the company, or information that, if released, will hurt someone else.

There's another really interesting way to create a method of reciprocity persuasion. It doesn't require you to send a physical object, it doesn't require you to spend any real effort, and it puts a different focus on sharing information. If done properly, it creates a desire to "return the favor" without the individual driven to know what had happened.

This implicit use of the reciprocity persuasion technique is to Reveal A SECRET. This little twist will build up the value of information that would otherwise seem very meaningless. It gives you the ability to deliver something very easily to another person and easily stimulate an urge to reciprocate (often at an unconscious level—it's just a kind of slipping through).

A great example is taking place every day in just about any restaurant. It's going like this: The waitress walks up to your table to take your order, bends down, looks about conspiratorially, lowers her voice, and says, "I shouldn't tell you this ... I would usually suggest the Salmon, it's one of our specialties, but today, the fish just isn't new. I'd recommend the Sword or the Ahi instead. Most people don't know this, but the Swordfish and the Ahi cost less, and you're getting a little better. Research studies have shown that the waitress is getting a bigger tip.

The second type of secret that you can share is something about yourself. This is a type of sharing, and it can create a strong desire on the part of the other person to share information, to open up, or to give back in some other way. You could say something like, "Let me share something with you about myself that I just told a few other people ..." Think of all the forms in which you could use secrets as a reciprocity persuasion technique in deals, agreements, or other styles of persuasion circumstances.

There will be little known, confidential, insider knowledge about the third level of secrets you might reveal. People are curious, and individuals love to be inside, to feel exclusive. If you have confidential knowledge you can provide ethically, and that's relevant to the person you're trying to persuade, you can deliver that and easily stimulate the urge to reciprocate. The cool thing is that it doesn't have to be groundbreaking, even though few people are aware that it will build interest. Make sure you let the other party know that the knowledge that is being given is exclusive. You might say something like, "I want to share something with you. I just found out, only a few people know about it, and it's only going to be shared with a handful of people ... (offer the information)."

Before we finish off, let me give a few short tips for using the strategy of reciprocity persuasion. If you are in a discussion, you usually want to trigger it upfront early. Reciprocity reduces stress, which you would like to see early on with just about every conversation.

Second, don't offer too big a thing. If you offer some sort of thing or even some information with a very large value, it could look more like a bribe and build resistance.

Subliminal Convince

In this modern world, the tools are the methods of subliminal manipulation. They help you gain a game-field advantage and keep you ahead of the game. Subliminal manipulation methods are your best mates, whether you're a salesperson, a girlfriend, a teenager, or even a regular guy trying to charm his way out of a speeding ticket.

Such hidden manipulation techniques come in various ways and are effective in specific contexts.

1: Association with the good or the good

Larry, 28, is a director of ads for a major appliance business. Part of his job is serving clients left and right. Larry doesn't often satisfy his clients in the workplace, however, he also sees them in prestigious restaurants. They eat, negotiate the contract, and he foots the bill at the close of the meal. No matter how pricey the meal is, Larry will be paying for it all (with money, of course, from the company).

It might not seem like an example of a technique of subliminal persuasion, but that's only for those who don't know this business. What Larry used was Community Law.

He needed to feel positive after the encounter with his customers. That's what explains the good restaurant, the good food, and the bill footing. His customers would then associate their encounters with Larry and the organization with which he works.

The enforcement of partnership rule is a very effective technique of hidden coercion. You should also use the partnership rule to your benefit. Always associate with good things, and others will also see you in that light.

2: To be a Friend

For decades, the law of friends has been there. It notes that generally, people will support others they consider as their mates. This rule, even though you are still employed, can be very useful. Many of the best company chances have come from relatives!

When you're a dentist, for example, and plan to raise your appointments, please let your buddies hear about it first. Even buddies who haven't seen you since high school would be more than willing to help. This is because you trust your mates, and what they can do.

3: Dissociation from the Negative

The law of disassociation is the total contrary to the law of association. If you can't afford to be seen in a bad light, then this is a covert persuasion method that could help you a lot.

I remember one incident in which disassociation law came quite handy. It had been the experience of a friend, not mine. Here is what he has told me in his own words:

"I had to face one of the grueling obstacles of any relationship, when I was still in college: meeting the father.

Things went smoothly at first until after dinner when we sat in the living room to watch TV. A fraternity dispute that broke out between two colleges was recorded by the local news station. One of them was my old alma mater. It couldn't be a bad time for that piece of news to come out.

Of course, the father knew that I was studying in high school, having already grilled me hours earlier. 'Does your school ever get into such difficulties?' the father asked. They don't always get into struggles. This one sounds like a single situation.' I replied."

Note my friend used the words "they." He even got rid of the father's notion of him becoming a hooligan by disassociating himself from the band.

Using methods of subliminal manipulation to your benefit doesn't make you an egoist. It just means you have a better picture of human nature.

CHAPTER 16
Q&A (NLP, PERSUASION AND MIND CONTROL)

Any athlete knows that before entering the competition, you must first align hours of training to be ready and give the best of yourself. For many, training is solely the domain of physical exercise.

Creating the conditions for sports success means seeking to put all the assets on its side, including mental reflection before action, and Neurolinguistic Programming (NLP) can help.

NLP assumes that an outcome is always linked to a certain context and certain actions. If a result displeases, we must modify the context, our actions, or both at the same time. Certain actions, effective in a context, can prove to be ineffective when the context changes. You have to be flexible if you want to achieve and maintain performance. From there, the method approaches the determination of objective by a set of questions:

Question 1: What do I want?

The answer makes it possible to concentrate all the resources, all the energy in a precise direction.

Question 2: Is my objective formulated positively?

If not, question 1 should be repeated until a positive answer is obtained.

Question 3: Is my goal achievable?

If it is not, there is either an overestimation of the moment's capacities, and the objective must be revised downwards, or an underestimation of the difficulty if the objective is placed too early. It is necessary to set short-term interim goals.

Question 4: Does my goal depend only on me?

If this is not the case, doubt and pressure settle because the objective escapes control and becomes random. Winning a competition is a random goal, not an objective. The question must be repeated: what depends only on me to achieve my goal? One or more sub-objectives are thus displayed aligned with the goal.

Question 5: Is my objective formulated with precision?

It is necessary to visualize precisely the path, the stages, and the result obtained.

Question 6: Could there be disadvantages to achieving my goal or advantages of not achieving it?

If so, you have to re-consider the initial objective so as not to unconsciously "scuttle" yourself. By anticipating obstacles, you become aware of the brakes that could turn into excuses to legitimize a failure.

Question 7: Why is this goal important to me? What will it bring me?

An unattractive goal does not generate motivation. There are direct and indirect benefits, positive consequences, and secondary benefits.

Question 8: About my objective, where am I?

Assessment of the current situation, inventory: results obtained, objective analysis of the strengths and weaknesses noted, measurement of the distance between the objects.

Question 9: What could prevent me from achieving my goal?

Anticipating obstacles prevents surprise or discouragement when they arise. This allows them to be accepted and you will be mentally prepared to face them. An unforeseen obstacle is always more disturbing than an obstacle for which we have prepared.

Question 10: What do I need to reach my goal?

Identification of the means to be implemented to achieve the objective: assess the actions to be taken, determine the material means necessary, schedule them over time with a daily work plan.

PRACTICAL WRITTEN EXERCISES (NLP, PERSUASION AND MIND CONTROL)

More and more people are leaning towards techniques such as NLP, the law of attraction, or even EFT, which allow them to go to a higher level.

However, it is sometimes difficult to get rid of certain limiting beliefs. Therefore, I offer you two exercises that have an extraordinary power in them to change your limiting beliefs into beneficial beliefs.

WHAT ARE LIMITING BELIEFS?

A limiting belief is none other than a belief that does not work to your advantage. Whether you are aware of it or not, you believe in certain things that sabotage you. Nothing is more normal in the society we live in, where we are constantly harassed by the negative.

THE LOGICAL PATCH

The purpose of this exercise is to apply a logical patch to your limiting beliefs. In IT, a patch is like an update or a new version of an application. Corrections are made to an existing version so that the application better meets user expectations.

The idea here is to apply a logical patch to your limiting beliefs so that they respond better to what you want.

The logical patch aims to rely on rational experiences and facts to prove by A + B that your belief is wrong and that an update is necessary!

So, you can overcome your limiting beliefs with logic!

HOW TO BUILD A LOGICAL PATCH

STEP 1: EXPRESS YOUR FEELINGS TOWARDS THE GOAL YOU ARE TARGETING BY IMAGINING IT ALREADY ACHIEVED

"I feel wonderful and deeply proud now that my business brings me 4000 euros a month by spending more than 20 hours a week."

STEP 2: EXPRESS YOUR PASSION

"My passion is to create and develop new things like companies that are close to my heart."

STEP 3: STATE THE LIMITING BELIEF (S) THAT PREVENT FULLY EXPRESSING THIS PASSION AND ACHIEVING YOUR GOALS

"The economic context is so difficult that it is extremely difficult to make a living."

"I probably don't deserve more than any other to succeed."

"I am afraid of the reaction of my loved ones in case of failure."

STEP 4: EXPRESS THE OPPOSITE OF YOUR LIMITING BELIEFS

"Many people succeed in this economic context."

"There is no reason why I should not succeed with my desire to succeed and act to the best of my ability every day."

"My loved ones love me as much in success as in failure,' or 'No matter what others think; I want to try my luck and give everything to make my dreams come true."

STEP 5: STATE WHAT FULFILLS YOU MOST IN LIFE

"I feel fulfilled when I think of my successful businesses."

"I feel fulfilled at the idea of trying and acting towards my dreams."

"I feel fulfilled when I think of the extraordinary people I meet in my professional activities."

STEP 6: STATE A SERIES OF INDISPUTABLE FACTS IN SUPPORT OF YOUR OBJECTIVE

"I know people who started from scratch started very good businesses."

"My loved ones have already supported me in difficult tests, and there is no reason why they should not start again."

"I have already proven many times that I am a fighter by winning such a competition, by succeeding with such a competition, by carrying out such a project within such a company, etc."

All these steps make it possible to build a logical scenario to build new beliefs. Your patch, therefore, consists of the following elements:

"If (passion) my passion is to create a profitable business in the tourism of small French villages ..."

"And that I feel fulfilled at the idea of developing a business ..."

"And that I feel fulfilled at the idea of trying and acting towards my dreams ..."

"And that I know people who started from nothing and started very good companies ..."

" And that I have already proven many times that I am a fighter by winning such a competition, by succeeding with such a competition, by carrying out such a project within such a society ..."

"So it makes sense to think that I am perfectly capable of creating this profitable business with the means I have and whatever the current economic context."

The logic patch allows you to update the limiting beliefs you have about your goals and replace them with better ones. You can put as many "And "as you want as long as it brings a positive element in your scenario.

Always remember to do this exercise for a specific purpose. By taking the time to do this exercise against different goals, you will see different limiting beliefs emerge, and you can take big steps forward.

It is not obvious that you will find all the resources to eliminate all your limits thanks to this patch because this exercise has a limit: rationality.

We cannot always explain everything with rational concepts. Unfortunately, the mistake that many people make is to think that we can explain everything rationally.

CHAPTER 17
CHALLENGE & IMPROVE YOUR MIND

Your success and happiness depend on your state of mind. What you think you will become.

Our mentality affects how we see the world. If yours is distorted, so will you and others. Our beliefs and thoughts shape our behavior, even if we don't realize it.

Developing the right mindset is crucial to success in life. Here's how to update yours.

How to improve your mindset and how important mentality is

A mental state is a mind-state. It is the sum of our beliefs, opinions, and thoughts about the world and ourselves that we have formed. It is the lens we watch our world through.

Our creeds and thoughts are shaped by our education, religion, education, and experience. Our mind is "settled." That affects our perception and our reactions directly.

Attitudes can shift, but they can adjust gradually. On the other hand, attitudes have a short-term impact. This is why they are easier to modify. Our ideology is profoundly ingrained in our values, and more work is required to shift it.

Your state of mind makes your interpretations and responses predetermined. It shapes the connection you have with the universe and with yourself. Choose your mental state wisely.

Your mind can help you or hurt you

The most popular mindset theory describes two types: growth, in contrast to a fixed mindset.

A fixed attitude is a belief that our qualities are fixed attributes which we cannot change. People with this mentality believe that only talent can lead to success. On the other hand, with time and experience, a spirit of growth thinks our intelligence can grow. This way of thought allows one to devote more energy-actions to contribute to improved results.

How to change your emotional state: The boundaries

A fixed mindset restricts our learning ability, while a growth mindset helps us to reach our full potential.

There are, though, many more types of mentalities. The glasses we use are influencing how we interact with our emotions. A depressive state of mind can intensify our depressive feelings and make us ruminate.

Our mentalities have two effects on us: they limit our potential or release it—just a few examples, how to improve your mind.

Binary thinking, for instance, forces us to consider just two possibilities. In terms of "one thing" or "the other," we think and see things from a right or wrong perspective.

You may add insight or confuse your vision with the attitude you use

The various mentalities

Let's look at the common kinds of mentalities. This is not an exhaustive list but a point of departure to help you think about the goals you use without realizing it.

How to change the state of mind... True or false versus open mind.

We like being right. The trouble with this form of thought is that we avoid paying heed to certain viewpoints. Instead of learning, we care to win the debate.

The propensity to follow facts that support our beliefs is "confirmation bias." The desire to always be right makes us reject facts that could clarify our viewpoints.

How to improve the success of your mindset

1. Get your mentals more conscious

Respect the reality that it needs change to the mindset. Start by being more mindful of your state of mind. What criterion do you use to see the truth when you respond to a circumstance or before making a decision?

Do you adopt a perfectionist mentality? Or a me-me-me version (and feel the world's about you)?

2. The eviting binary view of reality

Most of the mentalities go wrong. They force us to take a black and white look at the world. Binary thoughts create a false dilemma. When there are more, we act as if there are only two possible options.

Challenge your thinking on binary matters. Evite the tendency to divide everything into two categories: black and white, good or bad.

3. Offer attention about your convictions

Improving your mind-state requires reflection. Our mentalities are deeply ingrained in our beliefs. To change our mindset, we first have to look at our belief system.

What does it hold you back from? Will you endorse or exclude your beliefs? Identify beneficial convictions and communicate alongside non-believers.

4. (Re) define your lifelong purpose.

We like to be part of something bigger than ourselves. What is your life intended for? Track your location.

Make a measure of your success. What are the mentalities which will help you get there? Choose the lenses that will help you achieve your ultimate mission in life.

Your life's purpose is not about the destination. It is all about the trip.

5. Transform mentalities that are limited to liberators

Which mentality doesn't help you? It's not convenient to shift your attitude, so it's worth it. To upgrade them requires you to replace your filter with a new one.

Your mindset is the goal which filters the way you see yourself and the world around you. Change your mindset: turn your crippling convictions into transformative creeds.

CHAPTER 18
WHAT CONTROLS YOUR MIND?

You go back and forth between what your mind is trying to impose on you and what your heart wants to feel. So, you are not sure what to do: let yourself be guided by the emotions that spring up in yourself or listen quietly to your reason?

What is certain is that you would do anything to feel free and happy. You would get carried away without limits if you knew for sure that this is what you need. However, you do not know. You doubt your heart, which can take you to a place where you will suffer, and therefore your mind acts to avoid it. Which of the two to listen to? This is your current dilemma.

Know that for your future well-being, you will benefit from listening to your mind and heart. Yes, both. Both of them have things to tell you: each has its specific characteristics for understanding and acting in the face of the world.

What your mind has to say to you

When there is a conflict between the mind and the heart, many people try to take a stand. On the one hand, some believe that reason is superior to feelings because letting them carry ourselves makes us vulnerable. On the other hand, some believe that emotions are essential to love others, and that love is what makes us live.

The point is, everyone is partly right. The human being is characterized by reason and heart, and the two form a whole that cannot be divided. Separating them is dangerous: the mind would use logic but forget what you are feeling, while the heart would guide you but could be wrong because it would have no control.

If you don't know what to do, listening to your head first is a good option. First, because it is the one responsible for thinking, arguing, and providing common sense to your most intimate being. Second, because it is your mind that will bring this point of wisdom that you may lack.

What your heart has to say to you

However, if you have no choice but to tip the scales to one side, don't let your heart be the servant of your mind. Remember that the right answer is not always in the logic and that acting without agreeing with what you feel will get you nowhere. It is good to listen to what your heart has to say to you.

It may have been given the property of being blind, but, despite everything, it is the part of your body that knows the most. Have you ever heard this sentence, which says that reason ignores what the heart already knows in advance? The heart is, above all, a specialist in adrenaline, intuition, drama, love, and resistance. It will give meaning to what you do, even if you do not see any meaning at all.

Emotions are decisive in a rational process. It is said that it is our feelings that mark our path, but it is our head that chooses the best form to place us on it.

Calm, listen, precaution

The quiet, listening, and precaution must be the compass of your movements. Everything you need to feel better and refocus is inside of you. Certainly, there is surely a point where you agree with what is troubling you. In particular, keep in mind that you cannot know in advance what will happen, but you must not allow a decision to harm you in advance.

What is needed is to manage to give harmony to this confusion in which you find yourself. You can do this by listening, establishing priorities and values that bring you closer to where you want to go. Turning your back on your mind will not help you since you will face situations without any brake. And not listening to your heart will do the same: you will never understand why you are moving in one direction or another.

Subconscious Mind

Much of the information that we capture with the senses when we are small is registered and stored in our subconscious. Along with this sensory input, it also records the beliefs and expectations that we draw from. And, leaving childhood behind, all of the intellectual substance can affect our actions considerably.

Analysis has identified a broad range of brain waves that we can classify depending on their frequency: from the relatively small activation rates reported in a deep sleep (delta waves) to the higher frequencies registered during active thinking (beta waves).

When children get up, the prevailing rhythms of their brain move from slower waves to quicker waves, that is, from the subconscious to the awake.

Delta waves and the subconscious mind

From birth to 2 years of age, the human brain works primarily with lower frequency brain waves. Adults in a deep sleep are in a delta, which explains why new-borns normally cannot be awake for more than several minutes in a row.

Thus, they operate primarily from the subconscious. They hardly filter, distort, or judge information that they have obtained from outside. At this age, the "thinking brain" (neocortex) activity is very small.

Zeta waves

From 2 to 5 or 6 years old, children begin to show slightly higher EEG guidelines. Children who "live in zeta" are mainly linked to their inner world and live in a trance-like brain state.

They live in a world of the abstract and the imagination. They have underdeveloped critical and rational thinking. For this same reason, young children tend to believe what they are told (such as that wise men exist).

Phrases such as the following strike you at this age: Good girls are quiet. Boys do not Cry. Your brother is smarter than you. You cannot do this. You will be a failure. You're bad... These kinds of statements go directly to the subconscious because slow brain wave states are the realm of the subconscious.

Everything a child sees and hears is consolidated in the form of beliefs, and those beliefs are what will determine his behavior and his way of interpreting reality in adulthood.

So educating with that in mind is quite important. Now that you know he is responsible for this important knowledge.

Alpha waves

The brain waves change once again at a slightly higher frequency from 5 to 8 years old. The critical mind starts to develop, helping us to analyze and draw conclusions regarding outside life laws. Simultaneously, the inner world of the imagination tends to be as real as the outer world.

The children of this age group often have a foot in each world. This is why they love so many role-playing games. For instance, if you ask a child to play a swimming dolphin in the sea, to become a snowflake blown by the wind or a superhero to rescue someone, after hours, he will still be involved in this role.

Beta waves

From 8 to 12 years old and onward, brain activity increases, even at higher frequencies. These waves last into adulthood and increase to varying degrees.

The door between the conscious and subconscious mind usually closes after 12 years. Beta waves are broken down into weak, medium, and strong. As children approach adolescence, they transition from low-range beta waves to mid- and high-range beta waves, similar to those seen in most adults.

Now that you have a basic understanding of how brain waves function, you have to realize that all the knowledge processed by your subconscious mind during your first seven years continues to affect your life. But if you become aware of who you are and care about knowing yourself, you will be able to control and manage the form of this influence.

So, if you have children in your care ... be careful about what you tell them! Because they will believe it. Be very patient with them, and constantly tell them how valuable they are. Love them and teach them to love each other because it will be something that, in one way or another, will be present throughout their lives.

Subliminal Influence

A subliminal message is a signal or message hidden in print, video, or audio and is intended to be noticed unconsciously. A subliminal message is intended to convey or encourage a stimulus to a specific purpose.

America

Subliminal messages are widely used in America. In posters, in films, and audio (often short audio fragments), advertisers often use messages that try to influence and manipulate the unconscious feelings of the user. Often feelings of excitement, or feelings that prompt you to buy the product. After all, almost

90% of all observations are unconscious, and only 10% are aware. This would, of course, be the way for advertisers to respond to the unconscious and try to manipulate unconscious feelings.

In America, a rapidly growing market for 'Subliminal Advertising' has emerged. Every year, nearly $ 50 million is invested in self-learning audio CDs (for example, studies or languages). In addition to the teaching material, they contain subliminal messages that should promote the stimulation of losing weight, quitting smoking, self-confidence, and other needs.

In the 1950s, there was an investigation at the Fort Lee Cinema in New Jersey. During the films that were played, a short flash of 3 milliseconds flashed every 5 seconds with the words "Eat popcorn" and "Drink cola." After the study, the results became visible: 58% of the visitors got more popcorn, and 18% started drinking more cola. It later turned out that James Vicary (the researcher) had come up with all the results to promote the use of subliminal messages. Nevertheless, this event is seen as the beginning of the hype surrounding subliminal messages.

Also, some studies have shown that these unconscious messages do work. In 2008, 61 people received the text "Nipeic Tol" on a computer assignment every 23 milliseconds. Afterward, a questionnaire was filled in with questions about the assignment in question. One of the questions concerned a choice between the brand "Lipton Ice" or "Spa Rood." 80% of respondents chose Lipton Ice. Of the people who had not seen subliminal messages, only 50% chose the same brand!

At the moment, studies are still ongoing about the effect and possibilities of these hidden messages.

Today, since the agreement is tacit, it is much more difficult to release oneself from the power of the mind because very few people know that it is really happening.

Subliminal influence has become increasingly complex in the last decades, and thousands of studies have been done to refine the techniques. He or she should at least somewhat educate him or herself in advertising, politics, subliminal messages, covert hypnosis, persuasion, and propaganda to fight these influences and be in one's control.

Education is the first step towards freeing oneself from subliminal control of the mind.

CHAPTER 19
CONCLUSION

Neuro-linguistic programming (NLP), a branch of psychology practiced today by many specialists, aims to help us reprogram our brain and our behavior via language.

This specialty postulates that our brains' decision-making system is linked to evolution centered on the search for pleasure and the avoidance of pain. These pre-established decision systems determine a priori our present and our future. Fortunately, NLP postulates the very Sartrian idea that by modifying these preprograms, we can be in control of our lives. That we can feel good, improve our relationships with others, and arrive where we want—a real treatise on optimism, in short.

So how do you regain control with NLP?

The sum of these five elements (beliefs, values, references, questions, and emotional state) can push to act or to paralyze. Have you ever wondered why you dared not run for this promotion, apply for this business, write to someone to meet him, or set up this box, which is nevertheless a great idea?

"NLP allows you not to let thought programs dominate your present and your future. By changing one of these parameters, we can make a powerful change in our lives." - Anthony Robbins

This set of practices, used at work, and in life, therefore, makes it possible to tackle the blockages of our brain and achieve our objectives. It's a science that explains how the brain works and motivates our beliefs, speeches, and actions. Then we can adjust that to achieve our goals. You can also change a habit, control your emotions, or get rid of a phobia.

1. Change your thoughts to feel good at work

Due to evolution, we are formatted to focus on negative emotions. Therefore, the challenge of NLP is to reframe this state of affairs to produce more energizing thoughts.

The other fact to bear in mind is that all circumstances are neutral: we can choose to think about it as we want. For example, if you love to do your weekly reporting because it clears your head and shows you your impact, your office neighbor may be blowing because it bothers her. The same task—reporting—brings you radically different thoughts.

And precisely, by modifying what we think of the elements that hinder us in our job, we can modify the emotions that we associate with it, and therefore considerably reduce our frustrations at work. Here are some exercises to get you started.

a) Energizing words vs. limiting words

If we have to remember only one thing from NLP, our thoughts create our reality. And since our words are the materialization of our thoughts, they also shape our outlook on the world. It is for this reason that Anthony Robbins proposes to favor the "energizing" vocabulary.

Practice:

Make a list of the negative words you use and replace them with positive vocabulary. This will induce a change in your daily thoughts.

Examples:

"It's impossible" becomes: "It's a challenge."

"I am ignorant" becomes: "I learn every day."

b) The flip flop of thoughts

Once the energizing words are in place, clearing up your thoughts is key. It is sometimes enough to readjust your perception of a situation that is a priori negative to feel good at work.

Putting it into practice:

Make a list of phrases that run around in your head on annoying subjects, and then transform each of them into an energizing thought, which you will choose to adopt each time the annoying thought presents itself to you. Yes, it is a conscious effort.

Example:

Limiting thought: "My colleague dropped me again on the XY file, it's unbearable."

Energizing thought: "I took on responsibilities by managing the XY file from A to Z. I helped my colleague, who owes me a great candle and will lend me a hand if I am overwhelmed."

2. Improve your relationship with colleagues

The following exercises will help you make some adjustments that will allow you to improve your relationship with those you get on "moderately well" and strengthen your ties with others.

a) The mirror of emotions

"Look for the beam in your eye instead of the straw in your neighbor's," does that mean anything to you? In NLP, this is the concept of the "mirror of thoughts."

Wanting to control or change the people around us is pointless. A powerful tactic for separating ourselves from the criticism we make of our colleagues is to look for their faults in ourselves and correct them. Because, more often than not, this immediately puts an end to criticism and makes us more tolerant and empathetic.

Example:

Have you criticized your trainee for being disorganized? Ask yourself if your planning and records are kept as well as you think.

Practice:

Write down the judgments you make on a colleague who annoys you on a sheet of paper. Highlight the faults of this colleague you find at home and correct them.

Strange as it may seem, others often irritate us because we find in them something that annoys us, which makes us ashamed. Once we have corrected these corrected faults, our annoyance fades by itself, and the relationship is only better.

b) Suspension of the judgment

Even more effective than the mirror of emotions, NLP entails completely suspending judgment. Because this nasty mania brings nothing and can even serve us.

Put it into practice:

Identify your judgments and examine them. Ask yourself how they make you feel. And question them: do you have enough elements to formulate them? To thwart them, imagine what prompts this person to adopt such behavior and try to put yourself in his place.

And above all, every time we spot a judgment, we can block it by saying to ourselves: "Ah, hold a judgment! We said, stop."

Example:

"Marie is still making her favorite with the boss. It is pathetic!"

Stop! Making such a judgment does nothing for you. Not only can this make you feel uncomfortable, insecure, and even angry, but it will not change your colleague's behavior and will not affect her since you are not going to tell her. Instead, you may think that Marie has a super pleasant interpersonal skill that allows her to create quality interactions with people and try to take seed.

Concretely, it is quite possible to block a judgment and consciously modify the thought associated with it, and the more you do it, the more spontaneous it becomes.

c) Blocking jealousy with a bucket list

Jealousy can spoil relationships with a colleague. Higher salary, great responsibilities, long vacations... how to react in the best way to avoid feeling jealous and to keep relationships peaceful. As soon as you look at your colleague with envy, you can take this as a way of exploring yourself.

Practice:

Whenever you send someone down, put what they do on a list of things you too want to do later. And start thinking about when and how you will get there.

And above all, do not forget to rejoice for your collaborator, as he would rejoice for us. For example, to congratulate him on his business trip to New York, the 20% increase he obtained, or even a conference on his specialty in which he can participate.

3. Achieving your goals

a) Being able to count on yourself

However, to succeed professionally, you must also commit to being your best ally and keep the promises you make to yourself.

Putting it into practice:

On a week-long scale, always make sure to allow yourself the time necessary to put your commitment into action: go to bed early to have a good day at work, allow X hours for a personal project... When you fail to treat yourself as a friend, understand why without judgment. And then, "self-shake" if necessary to become more benevolent with yourself!

b) Stay focused on the result you want to achieve

The expressions consecrated "the universe conspires in" or "everything succeeds" suggests that some people would be more "lucky" than others and that succeeding would be easier for them. In NLP, luck does not exist.

"Our decisions are the circumstances that determine our future." This repeatedly demonstrates how successful people set a goal and do everything they can to reach it. And from there, and from there only, follows this impression of luck:

"Once you decide to prioritize a specific thing, you give it a lot of emotional intensity, and by constantly focusing on it, any resource that can help you get there is obvious."

To reach a goal, you must, therefore, focus on it and seize all the opportunities that allow you to get closer to it every day.

Practice:

List all the simple things that can get you closer to your goal and back-plan the steps that should get you there. At each stage, praise yourself for moving forward, then focus on the next.

In a word

NLP is, therefore, very effective practice for advancing our career in the direction that motivates us. "It is a powerful toolbox for managers, which helps them to understand their employees, to be truly caring, and to support them better. For employees, this allows them to develop new skills, to get out of their comfort zone, climb the ladder in their box, upgrade their skills or even get a better job."

NLP should be taught in school: "It would help everyone to develop more peaceful, constructed and harmonious relationships with others and with themselves."

On the other hand, for this to be effective, it is necessary to train regularly, even daily. Because yes, building your brain to be positive is a job! Another constraint that you will understand is an inner path that no one can follow for you. So, ready to practice these exercises to improve your professionalism... and personal life?

www.ingramcontent.com/pod-product-compliance
Lightning Source LLC
Chambersburg PA
CBHW071811080526
44589CB00012B/749